The Language Education of Minority Children

The Language Education of Minority Children

Selected Readings

BERNARD SPOLSKY, EDITOR

The University of New Mexico

NEWBURY HOUSE PUBLISHERS, INC.

Language Science
Language Teaching
Language Learning

68 Middle Road, Rowley, Massachusetts 01969

Library of Congress Card Number: 72-75496
ISBN: 912066-65-2

Printed in the U.S.A.   First printing: August, 1972

TO AVI

whose efforts to become bilingual
have added an extra dimension to my understanding
of the problems of minority children

Preface

The growing interest in the problems of children of minority groups in the United States has been accompanied by the publication of à large number of books and articles. Several good collections of papers on the specific topic of language education for such children have also appeared. The aim of the present volume is not to compete with them, but rather to gather in one small book a representative selection of some of the best work in the field. It is intended to serve as an introduction to a complex and important area, and will it is hoped be valuable to teachers and to those who are preparing to teach. Every teacher of language arts needs some perspective on a problem that some of his students will certainly face. Until elementary school teachers are able to recognize the special difficulties of minority children, there will be no chance of assuring them the equal opportunity for education it is agreed they deserve.

I am grateful to the authors and publishers who gave permission for including the articles reprinted here: detailed acknowledgments appear with each article. The completion of the editorial work on this book has been made possible by a John Simon Guggenheim Memorial Foundation Fellowship, which is gratefully acknowledged.

Bernard Spolsky

Albuquerque – Jerusalem
June – November, 1971

The Contributors

FRANK ANGEL
President
New Mexico Highlands University

JOAN BARATZ
Education Study Center
Washington, D.C.

EUGÈNE BRIÈRE
Associate Professor of Linguistics
The University of Southern California

MARY FINOCCHIARO
Professor of Education
Hunter College of the City University of New York

JOSHUA A. FISHMAN
Research Professor of Social Sciences
Yeshiva University
and
Visiting Professor
The Hebrew University of Jerusalem

A. BRUCE GAARDER
Assistant Director
Division of College Programs
Bureau of Educational Personnel Development
U.S. Office of Education

GRAEME KENNEDY
Lecturer in English
Victoria University of Wellington

ROLF KJOLSETH
Associate Professor of English
University of Colorado

DONALD M. LANCE
Assistant Professor of English
University of Missouri

JOHN LOVAS
Assistant Professor of English
Foothill College
Los Altos, California

JOHN MACNAMARA
Professor of Psychology
McGill University

JOYCE MORRIS
Assistant Professor of Elementary Education
San Diego State College

SIRARPI OHANNESSIAN
Senior Research and Program Staff
Center for Applied Linguistics
Washington, D.C.

BERNARD SPOLSKY
Professor of Linguistics and Elementary Education
The University of New Mexico

RALPH W. YARBOROUGH
former United States Senator from Texas

Table of Contents

SECTION THREE: LANGUAGE EDUCATION IN PRACTICE

Introduction

1. The Language Education of Minority Children

Bernard Spolsky

One of the main characteristics that distinguish man from animals is his control of language. Animals have fascinating and complex communication systems, but none of them approaches the power of human language. Perhaps as a result of the human infant's long period of dependency on his mother, language in man has evolved to its present ability to express the almost infinite range of human thoughts, needs, and feelings.

The first few years of every child's life are filled with the task of acquiring the skills and competences that are needed for social life. Of these, competence in language is one of the most crucial. Exactly how it is acquired we are only just starting to understand,[1] but what is important is the observation that every normal child, in every known society, gains control of the language of his environment. The pattern of development is everywhere the same, whatever the child's intelligence, whatever the social or economic or educational background of his parents. Meaningful speech begins when the child is about one year old. Two or three years later, most children have mastered the basic sound pattern and structures of their language. By the time he is five or six years old, a normal child is able to understand most of what is said to him and can make himself

---

[1] For a presentation of contemporary views, see David McNeill, *The Acquisition of Language: The Study of Developmental Psycholinguistics* (New York: Harper & Row, 1970).

understood not just by his family but also by strangers who speak the same language that he does.[2]

The importance of this observation cannot be overemphasized. Natural language acquisition certainly takes time and effort, as anyone who has watched a young child will agree, but it is virtually universally successful. A child who reaches the age of six not speaking the language of his surroundings is a rare exception indeed.

All this learning takes place without any formal teaching, as a result of a child's innate language acquisition abilities and his exposure to a language being used for communication around him. Without special lessons or drills, he gains the basic control of his language. It is usually only when he is five or six years old that society chooses to help him in an organized way. Formal education systems, wherever they exist, consider language education a central task; and even when they are not teaching language, they are teaching through language. But this language education does not start from nothing. When a six-year-old child comes to school, he brings with him as a result of a huge investment of time and effort in language learning a high level of mastery of at least one variety of language. He is then often faced with the task of learning the variety or varieties of language chosen by the school.

An educational system's choice of language is a complex matter, depending on the working of a great number of sociological, political, cultural, economic, historical, and other factors.[3] In a number of cases, the variety that the school chooses is the same as that spoken by its pupils. Take my own case. Brought up in New Zealand by educated middle-class parents, I came to school as a five-year-old not just speaking the locally approved variety of English, but already possessing a strong respect for the written variety that my school wished to teach me. In my case, then, there was no difficult transition between the language of home and the language of school. But for a great number of children, the situation

---

[2] For more details on child language acquisition, see the selection of articles in Aaron Bar-Adon and Werner F. Leopold, eds., *Child Language: A Book of Readings* (Englewood Cliffs, N. J.: Prentice-Hall, 1971).

[3] The field that studies these factors as they interact with language is sociolinguistics: for an introduction, see Joshua A. Fishman, *Sociolinguistics: A Brief Introduction* (Rowley, Mass.: Newbury House Publishers, 1971).

is quite different. For them, starting school means starting to learn a new language. The five or six years they have so far spent in acquiring competence in their home language seem wasted when they find their teachers, their school books, or their fellow pupils using a different language. For them, there is a language barrier, established by the school itself, that blocks their learning, discourages their efforts, and reduces their chances of success in the educational system.

When we refer to minority children, we are concerned with the problems of those whose variety of language is not the same as that chosen by the school as a medium of instruction. It might be a different language, as when Spanish-speaking children are forced to study in English, or a different dialect, or a combination. And the children themselves might be a numerical majority in the classroom, with their minority status established by the school. There are for instance many classrooms on the Navajo Reservation where over 90 percent of the children do not know a word of English, but where the teachers still present in English a curriculum prepared for speakers of English.

The basic aim of this book is to draw attention to the language barrier created by a school's language-education policy. This is an extremely important problem. Learning in school depends on interaction — interaction of the pupil with his teachers, with his books, with his peers — and all these interactions are mediated by language. School is not just a place that teaches language; most of its teaching takes place through language, and most of its learning depends on a pupil's ability to understand what his teacher says and what is in his books. Without communication between teachers and pupils, there is little chance of effective education.

There are a large number of children, it is clear, who bring many of their disadvantages from home. Whatever their inherited capacity may have been, early malnutrition and the poverty of their home experiences seriously reduce their chances for development. But it is just as clear that the school itself, when it fails to recognize the implications of the language problem, creates many more disadvantaged children. Inadequate and prejudiced views of the language spoken by their pupils provide excuses for lazy teachers and incompetent education systems, who try to explain away their failures by references to nonlingual children or inferior vernaculars or substandard dialects.

Whatever language goals a society may set for its schools can be achieved only if they take into account the language competence that the pupils bring to school. There is no justification for the myth that children of lower socioeconomic class speak no language, or an inferior one, or a debased and inaccurate form of the standard language[4]. Such children have learned the variety of language to which they have been exposed, a variety with as much semantic richness, structural complexity, and potential for communication as any other. If society believes they must also acquire some other language or variety, then the schools must develop sound and effective methods of language instruction. But this cannot happen until there is an understanding of the situation. The readings selected for this book are intended to help make clear the nature of the problems and to point the way to possible solutions.

How many children, it is reasonable to ask, fall into the group whose language is different from the majority? If we take the world as a whole, then we are in fact dealing with a general problem:

> Given a moment's thought it is quite apparent that most of the world's schoolchildren . . . are *not* taught to read and write the *same* language or language variety that they bring with them to school from their homes and neighborhoods. Indeed, if this phenomenon is viewed historically, then the discrepancy between home language and school language increases dramatically the further we go back in time into periods that predate the vernacularization of education and mass education itself.[5]

---

[4]This topic and its educational implications are discussed in a collection of articles edited by Frederick Williams under the title *Language and Poverty: Perspectives on a Theme* (Chicago: Markham Publishing Company, 1970).

[5]Joshua A. Fishman and Erika Luders, "What Has the Sociology of Language to Say to the Teacher," to appear in *The Functions of Language,* Courtney B. Cazden, Vera P. John, and Dell Hymes (New York: Teachers College Press).

Within the United States, the problem is numerically smaller, but has been greatly complicated by the fact that for so long it has not been noticed. It is only quite recently that much attention has been paid to the fact that there are languages other than English spoken in the United States, and that many children still come to school not speaking English. In 1966, two important books appeared. Reversing years of general apathy toward the language of immigrants, Joshua Fishman's *Language Loyalty in the United States*[6] documented efforts of various ethnic and religious groups to maintain their mother tongues. For the first time there was a full picture of the vitality of American multilingualism, although the trend toward gradual language loss was apparent. In the same year, Harold B. Allen completed and published *A Survey of the Teaching of English to Non-English Speakers in the United States*.[7] In the TENES report, as it is generally called, Allen gave details of the scattered efforts being made for children who come to school not speaking English, but, he pointed out, data on the number of children who needed such help were hard to come by; few schools or state education systems even recognized that the problem existed, or had data on it.

We can still only make estimates. To provide some basis, it is useful to look at some figures: the 1960 U.S. Census figures giving mother tongues of the foreign-born, Fishman's estimate for three generations of non-English mother-tongue speakers in 1960, and William Gage's estimate of native speakers of foreign languages in 1960.

Only languages where one of the estimates is over 100,000 are listed; forty or fifty other languages or language groups have fewer than 100,000 speakers each. The 1960 census reported a total of 9,738,143 foreign-born; Fishman estimated a total of 18,352,351 and Gage a total of 20,312,000 native speakers of languages other than English.

6The Hague: Mouton, 1966.

7Champaign, Ill.: National Council of Teachers of English, 1966.

Language	U.S. Census 1960	Fishman[8]	Gage[9]
German	1,278,772	3,145,772	4,072,000
Italian	1,226,141	3,673,141	3,718,000
Spanish	766,961	3,335,961	4,430,000
Polish	581,936	2,184,936	2,067,000
Yiddish	503,605	964,605	907,000
French	330,220	1,043,220	1,261,000
Russian	276,834	460,834	399,000
Hungarian	213,114	404,114	365,000
Swedish	211,597	415,597	364,000
Greek	173,031	292,031	188,000
Norwegian	140,774	321,774	364,000
Slovak	125,000	260,000	221,000
Dutch	123,613	321,613	329,000
Ukrainian	106,974	252,974	218,000
Lithuanian	99,043	206,043	165,000
Japanese	95,027	–	120,000
Czech	91,711	217,711	180,000
Chinese	89,609	–	118,000
Serbo-Croatian	88,094	184,094	138,000
Portuguese	87,109	181,109	166,000
Danish	70,619	147,619	64,000
Finnish	53,168	110,168	56,000
Arabic	49,908	103,908	36,000
Tagalog	–	–	115,000

----

[8] Joshua Fishman, *Language Loyalty in the United States.*

[9] William Gage, in *Report of the Special Subcommittee on Bilingual Education of the Committee on Labor and Public Welfare,* United States Senate, Ninetieth Congress, 1967, pages 414–15.

Speakers of American Indian languages are not included in the above figures. C. F. and F. M. Voegelin estimate that the following Indian languages have more than 1,000 speakers:[10]

almost 100,000	Navajo
30,000–50,000	Ojibwa-Ottawa-Algonquin-Salteaux, Cree
10,000–15,000	Eskimo, Papago, Teton, Apache, Cherokee
5,000–10,000	Muskogee, Keres, Choctaw, Blackfoot-Piegan-Blood, Shoshone-Gosiute
3,000–5,000	Hopi, Cheyenne, Yuman, Zuni, Santee, Tiwa, Yaqui, Crow, Ute
2,000–3,000	Chickasaw, Sahaptin, Tewa, Seneca, Northern Paiute-Bannock-Snake, Kiowa, Pima
1,000–2,000	Comanche, Towa, Arapaho-Atsina-Nawathinehena, Winnebago, Oneida, Tlingit, Mohawk, Assiniboin, Yankton, Aleut, Omaha, Cayuga, Fox-Sauk, Flathead-Pend d'Oreille-Kalispel-Spokan

The groups most involved in recent bilingual education programs in the United States are Spanish-speaking (Mexican-Americans in the Southwest, Puerto Ricans in Eastern and Midwestern cities, and Cubans) and American Indians. As John and Horner point out,[11] there is scant demographic information available on these groups. The Mexican-Americans are a fast-growing minority, with considerable recent immigration from Mexico. Of the 2,720,846 foreign laborers admitted or paroled into the United States from 1958 to 1967, 2,377,363 were from Mexico; and Mexicans made up nearly half of the 718,808 Spanish-Speaking immigrants admitted

[10]C. F. and F. M. Voegelin, "Languages of the World: Native American Fascicle One," *Anthropological Linguistics*.

[11]Vera P. John and Vivian M. Horner, *Early Childhood Bilingual Education* (New York: MLA, 1971).

into the United States from 1960 to 1967.[12] Increasingly, the Mexican-American population is urban and the proportion of poverty is high. The school dropout rate among Mexicans in the Southwest is one of the highest in the United States.

Two-thirds of the Puerto Ricans living on the mainland are in New York, where they form the city's poorest group, with high unemployment and limited formal education. The 1968 Annual Census of School Population in New York showed that Puerto Ricans made up nearly a quarter of the elementary school population; adding other groups of Spanish background, the figure reached 27 percent.

The Indian population is spread throughout the United States, reaching a total of about 600,000. There are federal reservations in Alaska (50,000), Arizona (85,000), California (40,000), Montana (22,000), New Mexico (57,000), North Carolina (40,000), Oklahoma (65,000), South Dakota (30,000), and Washington (22,000). They are all very poor: 50 percent of all Indian families have cash incomes below $2,000, 75 percent below $3,000. In 1968, there were 46,725 children in federal schools and another 100,000 in public schools.

These three groups, with their special combination of economic and linguistic problems, have been the focus of recent bilingual programs. They are clearly at the center of those whose educational difficulties are associated with minority language status. But as the data quoted earlier suggest and as the articles that follow will make clear, the problem is in fact much wider.

The purpose of this book then is to give a picture of contemporary concerns in the language education of minority children in the United States. The existence of the worldwide problem is mentioned in some of the articles, and there is good reason to agree with those who suggest that the United States situation is made clearer by looking beyond its shores.[13] It is hoped that the brief introductions to each article and the references in them will encourage such wider reading.

---

[12]Department of Justice, Immigration and Naturalization Service, Annual Report 1967.

[13]See, for instance, William F. Mackey, *Bilingualism as a World Problem* (Montreal: Harvest House, 1967).

This volume is organized in three sections. The first gives some background in the nature of multilingualism and the scope of the language problems of minority children in the United States. An extract from a Center for Applied Linguistics study of the education of American Indian children, edited by Sirarpi Ohannessian, gives an example in depth of the kind of problems they meet. A report of research by Donald Lance on the Spanish-English bilingual presents a picture of the complexity of the sociolinguistic systems with which formal language education must interact. To round out this section, Frank Angel points out that the problem is not just a linguistic one: in American society, cultural differences are often closely interwined with social and economic ones, and it is far from simple to separate one factor from the others.

The next five articles focus on aspects of bilingualism and bilingual education. Bruce Gaarder argues for the need to teach children in their own language and speaks of the value of bilingualism for the individual and for society. Evidence on the connection between bilingualism and thought is reviewed by John Macnamara. Senator Ralph Yarborough summarizes the arguments that led to the passing of the Bilingual Education Act. The various models of bilingual education are presented, from a sociolinguistic perspective, in an article by Joshua Fishman and John Lovas. The section concludes with a paper by Rolf Kjolseth, who asks whether American society is ready for the cultural pluralism inherent in some models of bilingual education.

In the third section, a number of more specific curricular issues are discussed. Mary Finocchiaro makes clear that teaching English as a second language is a central concern in the language education of minority children in the United States. An article by Joan Baratz reviews the difficult question of teaching standard English to Negro children. Joyce Morris writes about the teaching of reading, the area of the curriculum where language problems are often first noticed. And two papers deal with testing. Graeme Kennedy draws attention to some of the ways that standard tests unwittingly discriminate against minority children. Eugène Brière makes clear the difficulty of measuring the language competence of children or the effectiveness of language education programs.

The final paper returns to some of the issues raised in this introduction. It points out the contributions that language education can make and calls attention to its limitations in solving the many problems faced by minority children.

Section One

Multilingualism In The United States

2. The Language Problems of American Indian Children

Sirarpi Ohannessian

The languages spoken by American Indians have been well studied; indeed, the study of Amerindian languages has been the central activity of anthropological linguists for more than fifty years. But with rare exceptions, there has been little attempt to relate this theoretical study to practical educational needs. One recent exception was the study of the problem of teaching English to American Indian children, carried out in 1967 by the Center for Applied Linguistics under contract with the Bureau of Indian Affairs (BIA). The report was prepared and edited by Sirarpi Ohannessian, director of the Center's English as a Second Language Program. The extract that follows discusses the linguistic, cultural, and educational background of the study. It is based on papers prepared by a study group and especially on two papers by anthropological linguists deeply involved in contemporary educational problems of American Indians, Professor Oswald Werner of Northwestern University and Professor Wick Miller of the University of Utah.

LINGUISTIC, CULTURAL, AND EDUCATIONAL
BACKGROUNDS: PROBLEMS AND NEEDS

The term American Indian is loosely used for groups of people whose habitat extends from Alaska to Florida and from New York to California. The languages they speak constitute varieties which are more diverse than those of the whole of Europe, and the cultural patterns they present are so different that any generalization about them is very hazardous, since although diversity has decreased somewhat in the last three centuries, the variety is still very great.

Reprinted from *The Study of the Problems of Teaching English to American Indians,* prepared and edited by Sirarpi Ohannessian, Washington, D.C.: Center for Applied Linguistics, 1967, pages 10–19, by permission of the author and the Center for Applied Linguistics.

A. Linguistic Background

The number of distinct languages spoken by Indians in what is now the United States is difficult to determine because of problems of defining language versus dialect. Voegelin (1941) estimated 147 languages. The number has since been somewhat reduced because some languages have become extinct in the last twenty-five years. However, there are some 13 large and extensive language families in terms of the numbers of their speakers. These are: Eskimo, Athabaskan, Salish, Penutian, Hokan, Uto-Aztecan, Kiowa-Tanoan, Keresan, Siouan, Caddoan, Muskogian, Iroquoian, and Algonquian.

There are no accurate figures on the number of speakers of the various Indian languages, nor is there reliable information of the proportion of monolinguals in these languages, bilinguals (either in English or another European language, usually Spanish or French, or in other Indian languages), or nonspeakers, that is, Indians who no longer speak their tribal language. A shift in language is apparently taking place in at least some Indian communities, but at present there are few accounts of the settings in which Indian languages are used and those in which English is used, whether Indian languages are becoming less frequently used, and whether there are generational differences in language use and language fluency. A knowledge of these factors could have strong implications for English teaching.

The attitudes of Indians toward language and language learning could also have strong implications for the teaching of English to Indians. For instance, some (e.g., the Mojave) believe that the Indian child knows his language at birth; others believe it must be acquired through exposure. Many believe there is a relationship between race and language and that Indian blood is a prerequisite for learning an Indian language and hence, by implication, that it is difficult for Indians to learn English well.

Where English is the native language of Indian students, variation from the regional standard or nonstandard dialects poses problems for the teaching of English. There are no descriptions of varieties of English spoken by Indians. Some of the problems of Indians in isolated communities lie in their apparent inability to use more than a limited number of levels and styles of English. It would be important for English teaching to know what gaps there are between the English of urban and rural Indian children and what gaps there are between their oral and written levels of proficiency in English. The impression of the study group is that being monolingual in English, apparently a goal that some educators have set for Indians in the past, has not always solved the educational problems of Indian students.

Many more Indian children are said to start school knowing some English at present than did a decade ago. Interference from the students' native languages is the most prevalent and obvious problem, but interference from nonnative English learned from parents by first generation monolinguals in the language, lack of vocabulary and experiential background, and the often highly artifical usage of English in the classroom may be regarded as additional problems.

B. Cultural Background

Since language is found in a cultural and social context and forms a very important aspect of this context, it seems necessary, in considering the teaching of English to and the use of English by American Indians, to consider also the cultural factors that may affect language, language use, and language behavior. Perhaps the most important fact to bear in mind when examining the cultural background of American Indian education is that Indians are not immigrants to this country. The root and home of their culture is here and not in Europe or elsewhere, and they have fought bitterly against great odds to keep intruders out. Their resistance to assimilation into the larger American culture cannot be compared with that of others who have left the mainstream of their own cultures and freely chosen to live in a different one. However, in certain instances in the past, Indians have both accepted and resisted innovations brought in by the white man. They have, for instance, accepted the horse, literacy, and modern gadgets, but some have resisted assimiliation, as the Iroquois have done since the collapse of their tribal sovereignty some two hundred years ago.

Both acceptance and rejection of assimilation exist today, varying with the attitude of individuals and groups, and to a certain extent with the size of the group, proximity to communities of non-Indian culture, blood mixture, and other factors. Some Indians appear to be actively striving for assimilation and do not regard the culture of the majority group as one imposed on them. Others actively or passively reject it.

During their visits, the study group found limited interest in Indian culture and language among the staffs of the schools studied.[1] Where there was involvement of the Indian community in school affairs and an interest was shown by school personnel in Indian culture and language, there seemed to be both appreciation and cooperation shown by the Indian community.[2] In one school in which group members were able to observe a class on Indian culture, both non-Indian and Indian students, particularly the former, showed very great interest.

Some members of the group, on the other hand, felt that a basic lack in the education of the Indian student was that of background information on modern American life and culture. They felt that it was essential to give Indian students a perspective of the majority culture through an active program of excursions into it. Such perspective could better prepare the students to live in American society either as bilingual and bicultural individuals or as assimilated members. The schools were providing some rather stilted aspects of the non-Indian culture by turning their classrooms into typical replicas of others in the United States and by the use of materials prepared for the typical American public school. There were also activities connected with Easter and St. Patrick's Day; there were mixed dances arranged for the older students and excursions organized to metropolitan areas, but these seemed to be incidental and casual activities rather than a planned, systematic presentation of the culture of the wider modern American community. Educators and group members were in agreement that more was needed to give the students any depth of understanding of the many facets of this culture.

A number of teachers complained of the lack of interest,

---

[1]Of the 287 who answered the factual questionnaires, two non-Indians indicated they spoke an Indian language well, six understood one but did not speak it well, and nine had studied the structure of an Indian language. Of the twenty-two schools on the first list, one, a BIA boarding school, was experimenting with teaching the vernacular to a small group of children.

[2]In one BIA day school an education committee of Navajos was appointed by the chapter office and was doing very useful work as liaison between the principal and parents. In another an extensive, community-oriented program was being run under joint BIA and OEO funds.

incentive, and motivation to learn English among their students. The few contacts of group members with students, however, did not always substantiate this. Patterns of behavior, such as passivity, shyness, apparent lack of interest, distaste for public competition, and reluctance to excel in the classroom, may be attributed by teachers and other educators to lack of motivation. But this behavior may be at least partly rooted in other factors.[3]

One such factor may be differences in what may be called the respective styles of learning prevalent in the major American culture and that of some Indian communities. The first stresses learning by doing, whereas there is reason to believe that the second relies on prolonged observation, or "prelearning," which is then followed by learning. A reluctance to try too soon and the accompanying fear of being "shamed" if one does not succeed may account for the seemingly passive, uninterested, and unresponsive attitude of Indian students.[4] Understanding of the ways in which learning takes place among Indians may prove of far greater significance for the education of Indians in general and for their success in acquiring English in particular than elaborate projects based on patterns of learning behavior that are alien or even abhorrent to Indians.

Another factor may be the Indian cultural trait of non-interference. There seems to be general agreement among anthro-

---

[3] Three findings were obtained in the attitude survey that seem relevant to this paragraph. First, although it was true that the average response of the teachers was a tendency to perceive the students as not highly motivated to learn English, there were considerable individual differences in this attitude. Second, those teachers who felt that the students were not motivated to learn English felt also that the students experienced pressure from the peer group to avoid learning English and were faced with cultural barriers which impeded English acquisition. This pattern, moreover, seems more characteristic of some tribes than others and is, in the opinion of the investigator, an important observation. Third, when asked to characterize Indian students, the overall impression was highly favorable. Moreover, traits such as *active, interested, hardworking, honest,* and *peace-loving* were preferred to their polar opposites. It is true that polarity for these was not so pronounced as for other traits, such as *likeable, happy,* etc., but they were preferred. These would seem to disagree with traits such *passivity, apparent lack of interest,* and *delinquency.*

[4] A Navajo girl, for instance, is said to watch her mother weaving rugs for a very long time before she asks for a loom. She then produces a small rug of marketable quality.

pologists that for the Indian any form of coercion may result in bewilderment, disgust, fear, or withdrawal. Thus, coercion in the classroom may result in silent withdrawal, taking the form of nonresponsiveness, apparent indifference, laziness, or even flight.

Parental coercion of children in such matters as whether or not a child will attend school, what school he will attend, how regularly, and how hard he will work, appears to be minimal. However, group members were told this was changing. Parents now may ask the principal to send someone, usually the bus driver, to make children attend school.

Another factor affecting the success of some Indian students was felt to be their self-concept. It was pointed out that reservation experience, poverty, and assaults on Indian language and culture through the process of assimilation often adversely affect the self-concept of some Indians and prevent their achieving the goals that other students of their age achieve.

Some Indians seem to accept a certain amount of recklessness in male youth (the warrier syndrome) as a normal part of their preparation for respected manhood. Anthropologists indicate that the pattern of late education, evident in large numbers of older Indian students in school, may have been carried over into present-day life from tribal custom of certain Indian groups in the preparation of medicine men and warriors. Considering the apparently great number of dropouts both at the school and college levels, this cultural trait of late intellectual training may indicate the need for a closer look at the possibilities of special programs for older Indian students and adults.

C. Educational Background

Patterns of schooling for the education of the Indian child present a very complex picture. Indian children go to public, federal, and to a much lesser extent, mission schools. The schools they attend may be day or boarding schools or varying patterns of each. They may also be housed in dormitories and attend day public schools in the bordertown pattern. This study assumes that this complexity is in part due to the present transitional stage, when each year greater numbers of Indian children are entering state schools and the policy of the BIA "to turn over school facilities to public school districts as rapidly as there is mutual readiness and capability"[5] is being implemented.

A number of states have already assumed responsibility for large numbers of Indian students, and in addition to over 53,800 children in federal schools and housed in federal dormitories, the Bureau at present has partial financial responsibility for approximately two-thirds of Indian children in public schools.[6] If this trend is to continue, there is urgent need for long-term plans and a definite time schedule in consultation with state departments of education and the Indian community for the gradual transfer of Indian students to public schools.

Members of the study group consider it very important to make all long-term and short-term plans and goals clear to BIA employees. Channels of communication between the different levels of the educational hierarchy in the Bureau and within these levels need to be clarified and simplified. There is very little evidence of contact between principals in different areas or indeed within the same area. In one area visited, the last principals' meeting had taken place in 1963. Also there appears to be insufficient machinery in many areas for teachers to meet regularly with their colleagues from other schools and to exchange information and ideas. There is great need for closer cooperation among BIA personnel, between them and personnel in state education systems, and other federal projects now in operation.

As is to be expected, there are sharp differences of sophistication, training, and competence among teachers of English and other subjects in these schools.[7] Some excellent teaching was observed.

---

[5] *Report to the Senate Appropriations Committee on the Navajo Bordertown Dormitory Program by the Commissioner of Indian Education, February, 1965,* U. S. Department of the Interior, Bureau of Indian Affairs, p. 39.

[6] For a brief statistical and historical account see *Fiscal Year 1966 Statistics Concerning Indian Education,* U.S. Department of the Interior, Bureau of Indian Affairs, Division of Education.

[7] At present very few teachers seem to have had special training in linguistics or TESOL. Of the 216 BIA personnel who replied to the questionnaires, 3 had attended NDEA summer institutes for teachers of English as a second language, 21 had attended other summer institutes (mainly BIA), 25 had been to local or state workshops, and 18 had done course work in this field; 24 others said they had in-service or other training.

Where teachers are interested in language problems and have had some training and exposure to linguistics, it is reflected in their teaching. Many, however, display a great naïveté about language, a lack of awareness of problems of second-language learning, and modern approaches to these problems. Sometimes insufficient training and information cause a distorted interpretation of modern techniques, ending in their misuse. In some schools there is a very narrow interpretation of TESOL techniques, again with unfortunate results. An integrated approach to English teaching and a better realization that one of the most important aims of language teaching is to enable the learner to communicate in the language being taught need to be stressed. Almost all teachers and administrators, however, show a genuine and sympathetic concern about the personal welfare and nonacademic problems of their students.

Teacher turnover is a serious problem in some areas, and may need a closer examination than the present study can provide. Although some schools report very little change in the last two or three years, the turnover is 80 percent in some, and 30 percent does not appear unusual in others. Also to be examined are salary scales of the BIA in relation to the public schools; the longer school hours and shorter vacations for BIA teachers; the low salary ceiling which forces competent people out of teaching into administration; and living conditions in isolated places with little social life. All these factors need attention if teaching the Indian child is to be rewarding and attractive to well-trained and interested teachers.

On the whole there are fewer Indian teachers in the schools visited than seems desirable. BIA officials appear to be willing to hire them, but the scarcity of well-trained Indian personnel, tribal rivalries that may cause resentment at the appointment of members of other tribes, and other factors have made this difficult so far. One factor may be the Indian distaste for the "coercion" expected of the teacher in the American system of education.

School attendance figures reflected in the returns from question-naires[8] do not in general agree with the impressions of group

---

[8] In sixteen BIA schools, the average daily attendance was 92 percent and in four public schools 95 percent.

members that there is frequent and prolonged absenteeism among the student body. A child of twelve, for instance, was found in a beginning class in a boarding school, the explanation given being that the parents had not brought him before. Children may often be out of school for prolonged periods of time to receive religious training or to help the family by looking after sheep or to take care of younger siblings. Sometimes the reason seems to be simply that the child does not wish to attend school. These and other problems make it very difficult for the authorities to know how many and which children will be in school each year and to convey exact information on the schools before the term starts. This causes problems of adequate staffing, space allocation, and class scheduling for the heads of the schools.

In general, the performance of Indian students in standardized tests of all kinds ranks consistently below national norms. As reported in *The Indian Child Goes to School* [9] in 1958, the Indian child seems to fall progressively behind these norms as he goes up the school ladder, and the picture seems much the same today, particularly in English. The excessive amount of silent seatwork in class, the tendency of Indian students to be unresponsive, and the inevitable brevity of the group's time for observation prevented a systematic assessment of the oral English of students. There is serious need for an analysis of the trouble spots in the oral performance of Indian children and their attitude toward English.

The physical facilities in schools are generally very satisfactory. Classrooms are well equipped, well furnished, and sometimes even have tape recorders and television sets. There are, however, a few exceptions where old buildings, crowded classrooms, unsatisfactory office space, and unattractive grounds make a sharp contrast to the excellent facilities and very generous space of such schools as Chuska and Rock Point boarding schools. Boarding house facilities are good in general, though they, too, reflect differences in the allocation of funds evident in differences of space and equipment among various schools. One general observation is that there is often need for more

---

[9]L. Madison Coombs, Ralph E. Kron, E. Gordon Collister, and Kenneth E. Anderson, *The Indian Child Goes to School: A Study of Interracial Differences* (U.S. Department of the Interior, Bureau of Indian Affairs, 1958).

time and for more adequate, well-lit, and quiet space for homework after school hours.

Library facilities, for students and for teachers, vary among schools, but on the whole seem adequate in quantity, though the quality and variety of the holdings in some schools need improvement.[10] There is need in many of the libraries for materials on Indian language, Indian culture, and literature concerned with Indians. There is need for professional reference materials for the teacher, including up-to-date materials on the English language, the methodology of TESOL, and second-language learning, as well as periodicals in this field. There is great need for more opportunities for library utilization by students outside school hours.[11]

BACKGROUND TO RECOMMENDATIONS

At present the education of the Indian student depends to a very great extent on how efficiently he is taught English and how well he is able to learn it. Since all his other subjects will have to be learned through its medium, in a sense all his teachers are teachers of English. His higher education, again, is available only through the medium of English, and most of the careers open to him, as well as his contacts with the larger American community, are dependent very largely on his ability to communicate in English. The school, therefore, has a particularly urgent duty to equip him with this ability. The Indian community appears to realize the importance of education for its children and the vital role English plays in it.

Throughout the study, and in their personal and professional contacts with Indian education, members of the group were impressed with the present concern of the BIA with the language problems of Indian children, its willingness to face the tremendous

---

[10]Of the twenty schools responding to the questions regarding libraries, all provide reading materials to students either in the library (nineteen out of twenty) or in the classroom or dormitory, eleven provide special library periods for the classes, and all twenty provide materials for the leisure time reading of students. More fiction and periodicals seem to be provided for this than nonfiction, newspapers, or reference books.

[11]One school was using PL 89-10 funds to expand and improve its library and provide additional study space and time in the library for students after hours.

problems confronting it, and the flexibility it is showing in the search for solutions to these problems. The BIA is in an especially fortunate administrative position which allows it to take imaginative and vigorous steps towards the solution of these problems and the improvement of English teaching.

The present study is indebted to previous surveys of Indian education and the insights they provide into the many problems facing it, in particular to the long-range investigation conducted by Coombs, Kron, Collister, and Anderson and reported in *The Indian Child Goes to School.*[12] The basic problems are still much the same as those reported in this survey, but changes in the broad national picture, as well as those in the Indian community, reflect new attitudes and may perhaps provide a more propitious climate for the teaching of English.

In the last few years an increasing amount of attention has been directed toward the language problems of minority groups in the United States, chiefly through the availability of foundation and federal money for this purpose. Results of this attention are reflected in NDEA summer institutes for teachers of English as a second language; the greater number of seminars, workshops, and in-service training programs for such teachers; the production of instructional materials, such as the *Miami Linguistic Readers;*[13] and the activities of such programs as Head Start.

There has also been greater attention paid in university TESOL programs to the problems of children at the elementary and secondary levels. University programs themselves have increased. From 1960 to 1966 the number of institutions offering doctoral degrees with concentration in this field have increased from three to six, those offering master's degrees from eight to twenty-five, and while no bachelor's degrees were offered in 1960, there were ten

---

[12] L. Madison Coombs, Ralph E. Kron, E. Gordon Collister, and Kenneth E. Anderson, *The Indian Child Goes to School: A study of Interracial Differences* (U.S. Department of the Interior, Bureau of Indian Affairs, 1958).

[13] *Miami Linguistic Readers*   [Series produced under the Ford Foundation Project, Dade County Public Schools; Pauline Rojas, Project Director] (Boston: D.C. Heath, 1964).

institutions offering them in 1966.[14] There has also been more research and experimentation in this field in the last few years, and American institutions have gained much experience in the field through the training of such groups as Peace Corps volunteers.

These developments have had their impact on public school systems. There is at present a far greater concern on the part of state education authorities over the language problems of non-English-speaking minority groups. This concern is not uniform, and much remains to be done to make public schools ready for Indian students. Many schools are, however, actively working to solve the problems of their Indian and Spanish-speaking children and are far more ready for the responsibility of their education than they were a decade ago.

Two assumptions were made in drawing up the recommendations that follow. The first is that the education of the Indian child will eventually become a state responsibility and that the present trend of transfer to public schools will accelerate. Therefore it is important to bear in mind the present and potential role of public schools in Indian education.

The second is that at present a better understanding of linguistic and cultural relativity, among other factors, has resulted in a greater respect for and sympathy toward the language and cultural heritage of minority groups in the United States. It must be stated again that Indians are not immigrants to this country, the setting of their cultural heritage is still where they live today, and their problems are not the same as those of immigrant groups. There seems to be a degree of optimism among some Indians at present. The study group felt that the Indian community should be helped to become more aware of the general attitude in American society, as well as of the Indian cultural heritage, and be involved as actively as possible in the education of its young people.

---

[14] Sirarpi Ohannessian, "Patterns of Teacher Preparation in the Teaching of English to Speakers of Other Languages," *Selected Conference Papers of the Association of Teachers of English as a Second Language (A Section of the National Association for Foreign Student Affairs) 1966*. Robert B. Kaplan, Ed. (NAFSA Studies and Papers, English Language Series, No. 12), (Los Angeles: NAFSA, The University of Southern California Press, 1966), pp. 8–14.

3. The Codes of the Spanish–English Bilingual

Donald M. Lance

One result of the mixture of languages in the United States is often that two or more languages fill distinct and complementary roles within a single community. On the Navajo Reservation, for instance, Navajo is used for almost all spoken functions (at home, at the store, on the radio, at tribal council meetings), but English is used for any written purposes (at school, for signs, in the tribal newspaper, in official documents). Thus, while there are many hours of radio broadcasting in Navajo, the announcers work from scripts written in English, and while law courts hear cases argued in Navajo, their records are kept in English. In immigrant communities, there is often a distinction between the functions for which the old language is used (home, church, and community affairs), and those where the new language is needed (work, school, and contacts with the government). Often there is a difference according to age, with younger members of the community being more likely to speak the new language. For those who wish to learn more about this phenomenon, two studies can particularly be recommended: Einar Haugen, *The Norwegian Language in America* (Philadelphia: University of Pennsylvania Press, 1953), and Joshua Fishman, *Bilingualism in the Barrio* (Bloomington; Indiana University Publications, Language Science Monographs, 1971).

In the article that follows, which is a slightly revised version of a paper read at the 1970 TESOL Convention, Professor Donald M. Lance reports on a study of another group, Mexican Americans in East Texas. Professor Lance, previously at Texas A.&M. University, where he carried out this research, now teaches in the English Department at the University of Missouri.

This paper presents some conclusions that I have drawn as a result of a small research project conducted at Texas A. & M. University in the spring and summer of 1969.[1] The core of the investigation was a

Reprinted from the *TESOL Quarterly* , 4, 1970, pages 343–51, by permission of the author and the publishers.

[1] The project was funded by the Research Council of Texas A. & M. University. A final report, consisting of five papers and brief conclusions, was reproduced in a limited number of copies and given fairly broad distribution. The report is available from ERIC Document Reproduction Service as document number ED 032 529.

series of interviews with three generations of one family in the East Central Texas city of Bryan. Having grown up on a South Texas farm in the 1940's, I have generally found that my own ideas on bilingualism have seldom jibed 100 percent with the generalization that I have heard and read from my Anglo colleagues in recent years. Specifically, it has seemed to me that interference phenomena have been assigned too large a role in statements about the linguistic performance of Southwestern bilinguals, particularly in pedagogical studies. Thus, I wanted to collect some data and look for concrete evidence of, among other things, cross-code interference.

The research plan called for a graduate student and me to interview the three generations, with her interviewing them in English and me in Spanish; later the project secretary, a bilingual, also interviewed some of the informants. For purposes of comparison, another graduate student interviewed some foreign students in order to compare their linguistic competence with that of native bilinguals. Because of time limitations, the project was not large enough for the results to be deemed unequivocally definitive, for the sampling to be truly representative of bilingual communities in general terms.

In analyzing the informants' linguistic behavior, I have found it useful to keep in mind Chomsky's distinction between *performance*—that is, the actual use of language in concrete situations— and *competence*—that is the speaker-hearer's knowledge of a particular language.[2] As both the linguistic data and the personal experiences discussed here indicate, it is often difficult to separate completely the purely Spanish (code) and the purely English (code)—if they are indeed separable in bilinguals who have used the two languages since childhood.

The family chosen for this project, by chance rather than by design, displays the vast range of possibilites that exists in many bilingual communities. The family is more representative, of course, of communities with relatively small Spanish-speaking populations; along the Texas border, where the majority of the population is Mexican-American, the situation is quite different. Families with other educational and occupational histories would also be different.

[2] Noam Chomsky, *Aspects of the Theory of Syntax* (Cambridge, Mass.: M.I.T. press, 1965), p. 4

The grandmother and grandfather, both born in South Texas, never attended school and thus received no formal education in either English or Spanish. The grandmother claimed to speak no English at all, but it was obvious when I was interviewing her daughter in English that she understood much of what was being said. The grandfather knew enough English to make a modest living in a predominantly Anglo area, but after the first interview—which was in Spanish—he would not speak English with me at all, though we conversed freely on many different topics in Spanish. Also, when I tried to get him to speak English, he displayed as much discomfort as his grandchildren did when I tried to get them to speak Spanish with me.

The grandfather's overall linguistic competence, I must add, was more sophisticated than one might expect in the unschooled. He had learned the alphabet and could sound out words in Spanish, though not in English. Rather interestingly, he did not use some of the more obvious regional dialect forms that brand rural Mexican and Texas Spanish as substandard—namely, *muncho, pos,* and *pa'* for *para* in certain expressions—and he tended to enunciate more distinctly. Though we did not engage in secondary comments about Spanish, I suspect that he has a rather clear notion of "correctness" in the use of Spanish.

The second-generation informants consisted of the son of the preceding couple, his wife, and a neighbor. The son was not as readily available for interviews as were his wife and the neighbor, so most of the observations about the second generation are based on the performance of these two ladies. In the interview sessions with the three informants from the second generation, we talked very freely in English and in Spanish and even with a combination of the two languages. In the Spanish interviews, there were occasional lapses into English, but these consisted of only about 100 words in a total of 3,800. In the English interviews, Spanish was never used. Thus, with this generation, as the occasion demands, either English or Spanish can be used exclusively, though there is a perceptible tendency to rely on English, particularly when an Anglo is present. The tendency to rely on English can easily be attributed to the subtle factor of language dominance, but politeness—whether conscious or unconscious—must also be recognized.

One of the questions in mind for the project was how "pure" the informants' Spanish is. In analyzing their performance, I found that none of the adult informants displayed any degree of interference from English, though they of course used a few loan words—such as bísquete, mixteado, queique, yarda, weldear—but there were fewer of these than I had expected. I also found less nonstandard morphology than I had anticipated; and very interestingly, upon looking into such works as Lapesa's Historia de la lengua española, Menéndez Pidal's Manual de gramática histórica española, Santamaríe's *Diccionario de mejicanismos,* and the Royal Spanish Academy's abridged dictionary, I found that almost every one of the nonstandard forms is listed as occurring elsewhere in the Hispanic world. A few words such as *bolillo* "Anglo," *chance* "by chance," and *vista* "movie" were not listed as occurring outside the United States. The same kind of temporal and geographical distribution applies to nonstandard verb forms such as *dicemos, juimos, váyamos, hicites,* and *haiga.* The only element of Spanish grammar that may be undergoing a unique development in Texas Spanish is in the use of past subjunctive verb forms. More research needs to be conducted on the use of verb forms in the Southwest and in Mexico, particularly among speakers with minimal formal education in Standard Spanish.

The third generation presents a more complex picture. The group consisted of two girls, aged twelve and eight, and two boys, aged eleven and nine. Mrs. Smith, one of the graduate students, conducted three rather successful interviews with them in English and got very eager responses from all of them. They displayed no difficulty in understanding or producing English, though they spoke with what one would call a Spanish accent. This accent, however, does not result solely from the Spanish phonological system superimposing itself upon their oral performance. Their phonology consists of a combination of (1) certain interference phenomena such as difficulty with /s/ and /z/, and /č/ and /š/, and—a fact that is seldom even noted—the failure to lengthen vowels before voiced consonants; (2) certain exclusively English phonological features such as eleven vowel contrasts, diphthongization, and breaking; and (3) an occasional typically South Midland feature such as the merger of /ɪ/ and /ɛ/ before nasals and a retracted and rounded /ɔ/.

The nonstandard morphology and syntax produced by the children does not result simply from cross-code interference either.

Forms such as *maked, tooked,* and *jumpses* also occur in the speech of monolingual English-speaking children, though monolinguals seem to master such matters as tense and plural forms at an earlier age than these bilingual informants have. Their mother also used uncommon forms occasionally, such as *drinked.* Other nonstandard items can be attributed to association with monolinguals in the neighborhood. Some of these are the use of double negatives, *ain't they was, them guys, if it's a game* meaning "if there's a game," and *When we come he be happy*—the latter construction having been picked up from local Black English rather than the speech of local Anglos.

A realistic assessment of the children's competence in Spanish proved to be a rather difficult task. There is considerable secondary evidence that they can and do understand and speak the language, at least in certain social environments. The family speaks both languages at home, and apparently the children spend some time with their grandmother, who speaks no English. Also, their church services and Sunday School lessons are in Spanish. In interviews with the research team, however, their linguistic performance raised more questions than it answered.

Three interviews were held—or attempted—in Spanish. First, Mrs. Smith asked them to tell stories to each other in Spanish after they had shown considerable enthusiasm in doing so in English. All except the eight-year-old girl did so with the same enthusiasm but with less accuracy in detail. Because the interviewer, who does not speak Spanish, was present, they could not keep from reverting to English and tended to telescope elements of the plot while narrating the story.

When I attempted to engage them in conversations in Spanish, they would answer, though with some obvious inhibition, either in English or in a mixture of the two languages. During all of our visits to their home, however, they had displayed very few inhibitions in talking with me in English. When I attempted to record their Spanish, the inhibitions grew so strong that they were practically mute. Not wanting to torture them, I abandoned the idea of a taped interview and talked (in English) with the eleven-year-old boy about why he would talk with me in English but not in Spanish. His explanation was forthright and simple: "It's too hard." He meant that the difficulty arose in speaking Spanish with an Anglo, because he further said that it would be easier to talk Spanish with Miss Reyna, the project secretary, if she were his teacher than with me if I were his teacher, though he could talk Spanish with either of us in such a situation.

Miss Reyna also interviewed the children. She had eminently more success than I, but they did not talk as openly with her as they had with Mrs. Smith in the English interviews, perhaps because they associated Miss Reyna more directly with the university, a more distant element of the "establishment." On our first trip to their home, they had recognized Mrs. Smith as one of the former teachers—and a favorite—of their sixteen-year-old aunt in the junior high school which they would attend later on.

Even with Miss Reyna, they displayed a marked tendency to lapse into English. The twelve-year-old girl obviously liked both inter- viewers personally, and her performance indicated a very strong urge to use the native language of the interviewer. In telling her story for Mrs. Smith, she reverted to English for 43 percent of her words, though she was obviously trying to accommodate the request for Spanish. On the other hand, when she was talking with Miss Reyna, only 4 percent of her words were in English. The eleven-year-old boy, who was a first-string pitcher for his Little League team, seemed incapable of suppressing English words and constructions in either of the interviews. In telling his story, he used 34 percent English and in talking with Miss Reyna he used even more, 42 percent. The nine-year-old boy was quite eager to tell his story and was more successful in staying in Spanish: he lapsed into English for only 7 percent of his words, and a good many of these were repetitions of *bear*, since he did not know the word *oso*. He was ill on the day of Miss Reyna's interviews, and one can only speculate on how he would have responded to her. The eight-year-old girl flatly declined to tell a story in Spanish and was reluctant at first to talk Spanish with Miss Reyna, but as the interview progressed she contributed more and more, with only 30 percent of her words being in English—a considerably smaller percentage than her older brother had used.

In reviewing the foregoing observations, one can see that in a manner of speaking the three generations of this family reflected a cultural development that has been taking place at a rather rapid pace in the Southwest since 1940, particularly in areas where the Spanish-speaking population is very much in the minority—between 5 percent and 10 percent in that particular part of Texas. Generation by generation, the individuals and families are developing a stronger "Anglo" dominance, linguistically and culturally.

The matter of language dominance can be seen most clearly in the relative amount of English and Spanish used when a bilingual speaker freely switches from one language to the other in relaxed conversation. In the Spanish interviews, the hostess lapsed into English 4 percent of the time, her husband did so less than 1 percent, and the neighbor 3 percent; whereas the children lapsed into English 4 percent, 30 percent, and 42 percent in the interview with Miss Reyna. These figures indicate some tendency in all these speakers to rely on English as the stronger element in their linguistic competence. In two interviews, I recorded conversations in which the two ladies and I simply talked, using English or Spanish or a mixture, depending on the word or construction that was "closest to the tip of the tongue." In these interviews, the hostess used Spanish 38 percent of the time, the neighbor—surprisingly—only 11 percent, and I only 21 percent. Suspecting that my presence had inhibited the use of Spanish, I left the room and asked the two ladies to continue freely mixing the two languages. Though both insisted that my presence had had no influence, their use of Spanish increased very significantly—more than doubled. The hostess used 71 percent Spanish and the neighbor increased her Spanish from 11 percent to 42 percent.

In referring to a "mixture," I am not alluding to the adaptation of English words to Spanish phonology and morphology. That is borrowing, as in the use of words like *weldear, mixteado, greve, bísquete,* and *parquearse.* The mixing of the two codes (more commonly, and more appropriately, termed 'code switching') is illustrated in the following excerpts from the interviews:

> Las tortillas se las venden en . . . let's see, I think it's a dozen for fifteen, las dos docenas por thirty. En el paquete. En las tiendas están más caro. Me parece dieciciete o dieciocho.

> Y una vez me dijo mi chamaca, dijo, "Mami, you go there order me a hamburger basket deluxe." "Are you sure que hay

asina, porque no en todos hay?" Dijo, "sí nomás diles que quieres un hamburger basket deluxe." Primero they were leadin' diez pa' nada. Then there was our team to bat and we made . . . 'cimos doe carreras. And then ellos fueron a batear. Hicieron una and then nojotros 'cimos cinco. Después 'ciron six, 'ciron cinco. And then they made dos and it was our time to bat and we made . . . ah . . . five or six. And they beat us by five runs.

The difference in the performance of the two women in switching between English and Spanish can be explained in terms of their personal history. The hostess grew up using only Spanish at home, but she works as a maid and has to take messages on the telephone, thus coming to depend on English as the sole or principal medium of communication on the job. The neighbor has a rather unique history. When she was six or seven, her mother died and her father married an Anglo. She then had to speak only English until her marriage at the age of seventeen. She relearned Spanish in order to communicate with her in-laws but continued to use English in her own home. thus, she is now definitely English-dominant, but even so she has virtually complete control over the Spanish language, as is indicated by her using English only 3 percent of the time in the Spanish interview with me. Her Spanish is without a trace of English interference, and her English is rather unusual for a Mexican American: phonologically and morphologically it is that of the East Central Texas rural Anglo, no doubt very much like that of her late stepmother.

Judging from the way in which these three generations of informants used both English and Spanish in talking with me, with Mrs. Smith, with Miss Reyna, and with each other, one cannot simply say that Spanish-English bilinguals have internalized two distinct and totally separate language codes, each one more or less completely. Instead, their Spanish and English together constitute their linguistic competence in a *singular* sense, and their linguistic performance can draw primarily upon English, primarily upon Spanish, or upon a willy-nilly mixture of the two. This same statement of course can be made of a number of other ethnic groups on this continent whose families use two languages: Yiddish-speaking bilinguals, French Canadians, Polish Americans, Ukranian Canadians, Czech Americans, and Norwegian Americans. In his discussion of code switching and borrowing in the speech of Norwegian Americans, Einar Haugen makes the following statement:

> In becoming bilinguals they were so to speak grafting a new stem on an old tree, and their further development proceeded partly in obedience to the habits of the old language, but much more in response to those of the new.[3]

In applying Haugen's metaphor to the informants of our project, one might make the following generalizations: the grandfather's linguistic tree has a limited number of English graftings, but the original trunk and branches are the only parts in which the grain runs true; his daughter-in-law has grafted together two trunks, one for the job and one for the family; the neighbor performed a major graft at the age of seven so that the trunk of her tree is basically English, but she later grafted on a major Spanish component which grew well because there was still a trace of Spanish sap in the adopted English truck; the twelve-year-old girl, for the time being at least, has two separate trees available and can build tree houses in one or the other depending on the native tongue of her playmates; and the eleven-year-old boy has begun to show a distinct affinity for the tree from which Little League bats are made, and in Bryan, Texas, it is an Anglo-Saxon rather than a Hispanic Tree.

(It would perhaps be of interest to the reader to classify the linguistic behavior of these informants in accordance with some of the more detailed theoretical discussions in the literature,[4] but since the sampling of informants and the data in the project are rather limited, I do not feel that such a classification would add substantially to the principal concerns of this paper.)

For purposes of comparison, Mrs. Ward, the other graduate student on the project, interviewed some Spanish-speaking foreign students on campus. In analyzing her data, she used a tentative unpublished analysis by Gustavo González, of the Southwest Educational Development Laboratory, of the English of a group of

---

[3] Einar Haugen, *The Norwegian Language in America,* I (Philadelphia: University of Pennsylvania Press, 1953), p. 52.

[4] Cf., for example, Joshua Fishman's discussion of coordinate and compound bilingualism in "Language Maintenance and Language Shift As a Field of Inquiry," in *Language Loyalty in the United States* (The Hague: Mouton, 1966), pp. 424–458.

twenty-six migrant children who had been learning English for slightly less than one academic year. Three of the foreign students had begun their study of English only one year before the interviews.

The most significant finding in her study is that the two groups of students tended to make completely different types of errors. The most common error among the migrant children was the use of the unmarked verb form with third person singular subjects, as in *he say*. Twenty-two of the twenty-six children made this error at least once, whereas the mistake was made by only one of the four foreign students, and only once. On the other hand, the highest incidence of errors among the foreigners was in the treatment of count versus noncount and singular versus plural nouns, whereas these were among the lowest frequency errors made by the migrant children.

One of the interesting sidelights of Mrs. Ward's study is that the double negative, which one would expect to be a common error among Spanish speakers, did not occur a significant number of times in the speech of either group of informants. In the Gonźalez study, this error was not listed as occurring in the speech of any of the twenty-six migrant children. And only two of the four foreign students used the construction, each using it only once. Thus, the tendency to use the Spanish double negative pattern in English apparently is rather easily suppressed. Further, if a Spanish speaker uses it at all, the influencing factor seems to be association with monolinguals who use it, for the construction is widespread throughout the speech of Anglos, Negroes, and Mexican Americans in Bryan.

The implications of the findings of this brief research project—for me at least—are manifold as far as future research and public education are concerned. The Spanish of the Southwest needs to be studied as a part of a broader analysis of Mexican, or North American, Spanish, including such matters as borrowing and the historical provenience and geographical distribution of nonstandard forms—for example, the fact that *semos* and *haiga,* rather than being modern corruptions, go back to medieval times. Menéndez Pidal points out that *semos* can be traced all the way back to Augustus Caesar's use of *simus* instead of *sumus* in the first century B.C.[5] As

---

[5] R. Menéndez Pidal, *Manual de gramática histórica española,* 11th ed. (Madrid: Espasa-Calpe, 1962), p. 302.

well, the English of bilinguals needs to be studied as a distinctive variety of *English*—a dialect—rather than as a hodgepodge of forms that illustrate interference phenomena.

As far as public education is concerned, more attention must be paid to the age of the individual who is learning the second language. As the study of the English of the foreign students indicates, the grammatical distinctions that cause trouble for first graders are not the same ones that cause trouble for college freshmen. And in view of the recent findings of Eric Lenneberg, this difference should not be too surprising. As he says, "There is evidence that the primary acquisition of language is predicated upon a certain developmental stage which is quickly outgrown at the age of puberty."[6] Thus, different instructional techniques and a different organizational pattern of grammatical data are needed for, say, six-year-old learners and fifteen- or eighteen-year-old learners of a second language.

One should not overgeneralize in regard to the linguistic competence or performance of individual bilinguals—particularly when they are children. As the eleven-year-old boy's performance indicates, if he were placed all of a sudden into a bilingual instructional program, he would have to undergo a considerable amount of internal adjustment. His strong tendency to choose English over Spanish when talking to me, to Mrs. Smith, or to Miss Reyna suggests that he would not necessarily view instruction in Spanish as an easy intellectual task—but perhaps even as an undersirable one. On the other hand, the ease with which his older sister responded to Miss Reyna suggests that she would adjust rather easily to a bilingual program. The situation is less clear for the two younger children because we did not get enough data from them. Further, if Anglo teachers are involved, the adjustment process will become more complex.

In the case of the children in this family, their contact with the surrounding community as a whole has apparently conditioned them to consider English as the appropriate medium of communication outside the immediate family environment, and any deviation from this expectation is so anomalous as to impede natural linguistic performance on their part. In making these observations, I do not

---

[6]Eric H. Lenneberg, *Biological Foundations of Language* (New York: Wiley, 1967), p. 142.

mean to imply that bilingual or bicultural programs would be beset by insuperable obstacles or would be less than desirable—only that many school children with Spanish surnames have developed cultural orientations that do not fit neatly into stereotyped categories. School populations in the Southwest simply are not globally differentiable, linguistically and culturally, into two separate groups, the Mexican-American and the Anglo—not even in the same family. The "codes" of the language-using organism, one must recognize, are essentially only theoretical constructs devised to account for the linguistic performance of individuals or groups; what *really* exists in a bilingual speech community is a collection of discrete human beings, each of whom has a single mind—i.e., a central nervous system— which "contains" Spanish-language and English-language behavioral patterns and "behaves" in accordance with the apparent require- ments of the immediate environment, producing a particular lan- guage or a mixture of linguistic items as prior experience with the social milieu has conditioned the human organism to do. In the American Southwest there are, then, individuals with varying degrees of Mexican or Anglo identificational patterns, and these genuine human responses must be respected as such.

4. Social Class or Culture? A Fundamental Issue in the Education of Culturally Different Students

Frank Angel

The primary focus of this volume is on language, but it would be a serious mistake not to realize that the language problem is part of a more complex set of nonlinguistic ones. A lifetime of concern for education in the Southwestern United States and extensive experience in Latin America qualify Dr. Frank Angel, now President of New Mexico Highlands University to pose the question: To what extent are minority students' difficulties a result of linguistic or cultural differences, and to what extent should they be attributed to social or economic factors? In any case, how is the fact of difference to be translated into classroom practice?

We have come a long way in our thinking about the education of students who are not members of the majority culture in the United States. This is true in New Mexico too. Building on the foundation laid by Tireman and Marie Hughes in the thirties, we have developed an approach that recognizes the existence of a number of factors other than language. Unfortunately, the progress in theory has not been matched by similar progress in practice, which continues to lag behind. Even in theory, some people are at a less sophisticated stage. Some still explain poor school performance by Spanish-speaking and Indian students as a result of language; their only proposal is to teach English as a second language. Others go further than this and propose teaching the native language, Spanish for Spanish-speaking

Printed with the author's permission, this is a revised version of an address delivered to the second annual convention of the New Mexico Association for TESOL and Bilingual Education held at Las Cruces, April 1971.

children and Navajo for Navajo-speaking children. Many others, judging from the present deluge of publication, find in socio-cultural-political factors the explanation of the Mexican American's disadvantaged social position.

Within professional education itself, there is at present some broadening of consideration of the factors linked with the socio-cultural environment—concerns that go beyond the psychology of classroom behavior. These newer concerns do not stop with the linguistic aspects of the problem, but add a number of additional interests: they look at learning and learning styles and how these might be conditioned and influenced by culture; they study the affective development of culturally different students and how this differs from middle-class and majority culture students; they investigate the implication of newer concepts of intelligence and their impact upon pedagogical practices. Other educators point out the implication of research on the teaching of thinking for teaching culturally different students. Attention has also been drawn to the effect of early nutrition—and especially of amino acids (proteins) on brain growth and development. And the question is being studied of the relation of motor skills and intelligence, looking at the positive correlation between high competence in motor skills and intelligence.

Some of these new thoughts may lead nowhere; others may prove to be productive and helpful. The main point I want to make in citing them is that the focus in the education of minority groups in New Mexico must be wider than that implied by the term "bilingual education," or even by terms like "culturally different," "disadvantaged children," or "compensatory education."[1] Such labels tend to narrow our thinking to the variables named. I would propose that we use rather the term "the education of minority groups." However, even this phrase might be too limiting for those of us who are concerned with the total life of minority groups.

I have started with this background because I want to deal with an educational problem that has broader linkages than the classroom. I would like to explore with you what seems to me to be a fundamental problem in the education of the Spanish-speaking and

---

[1] Terms which not only limit the focus but imply superiority of the majority culture and inferiority of the minority.

Indian students in New Mexico. In order to improve the school performance of the minority student should we focus on factors associated with poverty and lower social class membership or are cultural factors more important? I hope that such an analysis will provide us with insights that will be helpful to us as teachers.

My own examination of the problem was set off by a student teacher in a "cultural awareness" workshop. I had presented some of the implications of Piaget's theories on the development of intelligence for teaching the Mexican American. In the discussion, the student said, "I think all of this is very interesting. I think you have succeeded in making me culturally aware. I am very sympathetic with the plight of the Mexican American and feel no prejudice against him. However, as a teacher, I want to know what to do *differently* for the Mexican American child from what I do for the Anglo child when I am teaching him 2 + 2 = 4."

After a great deal of intellectual toe dancing, we somehow gave her an answer. I'm sure that she was not satisfied. The fact was that we could not answer her question from the kind of theoretical position we were maintaining. We went up and down the transcultural continuum; we talked about stages of child development; we talked about the relation of concepts to language; we talked about task analysis and entry behavior and preparing the child for the lesson objective; we talked about language facility. But we couldn't be precise. In subsequent weeks I thought a great deal about her question, and how important it is. If we can't show teachers what they should do differently with culturally different children when they get down to specifics in the everyday work of the classroom, is it because culture does not make this kind of difference? This is, in effect, the real test of the validity of what we have been sponsoring for the past twenty-five years.

Perhaps we are caught in a dilemma of our own making — perhaps continuing to emphasize cultural differences leads nowhere, pedagogically speaking. Are we on sounder ground in approaching the teaching problem in terms of diagnosing pupil entry behavior for a particular lesson objective and developing the appropriate teaching strategy to induce the learning we want to take place? Does culture enter into the teaching and learning picture as a generalized or attitudinal variable and not in specific terms, or in ways which we cannot specify with our present knowledge? Would we help the boys and girls in our schools more if we concerned ourselves with compensating for the erosion and psychological damage caused by poverty and lower social class membership? In short, is the basic problem in improving the education of Spanish-speaking and Indian children a matter of social class or of culture?

Why is this question so important? If, in effect, the school performance of Spanish-speaking and Indian students is due to cultural factors and influences and their impact on intellectual, affective, and psychomotor behavior, it is essential for teachers to modify their teaching accordingly. The puzzle has been how to relate culture to teaching practices on the one hand, and to learning on the other. The problem is not that we have focused on the *teacher* too much in the past and have neglected the *learner*, as some people believe, but rather that we have ignored the *processes of teaching and learning*. It is relatively easy to ferret out culture and its impact on teachers as people and learners as people; but it is very hard to trace its impact on the processes. When one considers the teaching and learning of math, social studies, and natural sciences, what should the good teacher do differently for a culturally different child than for an Anglo child? Sensitivity to the fact that there are these cultural differences is not enough.

A good teacher, for example, is one who is concerned not only with the acquisition of knowledge by the student but also with the affective component of teaching and learning, and who additionally takes a student's learning style into consideration. A good teacher recognizes that the child is a Mexican-American or an Indian, and prefers a curriculum based on cultural plurality to a monolithic one. What more is there? How differently should the teacher behave if she is working with a culturally different child? The burden of an explicit answer is on those of us who have sponsored the notion of cultural differences.

It is relatively easy to identify cultural differences in curriculum matters. For example, we have shown that the typical school curriculum has neglected the Hispanic and Indian and Negro cultural heritage. There are many unresolved problems in this area, but in general terms, it is clear what the school should do. All curricular areas will profit from the addition of cultural materials from Hispanic, Indian, and Black cultures, including math. The Iberic peoples through the Moors introduced mathematics to Europe and through Europe to America. The inclusion of the teaching of Spanish in the elementary, junior, and senior high schools as both an object of study and as a means of instruction is another element that derives from culture.

It is relatively easy also to see the implications of demands for equality in economic, political, and social affairs. Perhaps cultural differences are significant for curriculum and for social equality only, and not for the teaching and learning processes?

It is even easier to see the impact of social-class differences on teaching and learning. There is an ever-growing amount of research and experimentation regarding the impact of poverty on the intellectual, emotional, and physical development of children. What is now known about cognitive development during infancy and early childhood, what is known about amino acid deficiency, what is known about effective teaching and learning, what is now known about lower-class family dynamics, the known need for including intergroup relations and experiences, if applied, would improve the learning picture of the Spanish-speaking and the Indian students enormously.

A recent review of work dealing with the disadvantaged child[2] identified three major criteria in which the lower-class child is different from the middle-class child. Assuming there is stability on the affective side of his life, Wilhelms says, there are three things a child needs for his cognitive development: stimulation from his environment, full and well-articulated verbalization, and a rich variety of experiences leading to sensory sharpening. Homes seem to vary in these factors according to social class.

The knowledge gained from experience in the education of disadvantaged children and from compensatory education have fundamental applications to the education of the Spanish-speaking, Indian, and Negro lower-class student.

One wonders whether our so-called "bilingual problem" is not primarily one of equality rather than one of culture. The information showing the impact of lower-class membership upon students is increasing in both quantity and quality. We could do worse than to

---

[2] Fred T. Wilhelms, *The Influence of Environment and Education,* National Association of Secondary School Principals, April 1969, pp. 1–36.

apply this new knowledge. If we had the same kind and quality of research and experimentation regarding the impact of culture, perhaps we could more easily determine what to do, but researchers and theorists have not given the same amount of attention to cultural differences that they have to social-class factors. It seems to me therefore that before we discard the culture concept and its applications to education, we should look at it more carefully than we have done. One of the problems involved is disentangling *culture* and *society*. As David Bidney says,[3] "Culture as conceived is inseparable from the life of human beings in society; it is a mode of social living and has no existence independent of the actual groups to which it is attributed." According to Biesanz,[4] "Culture is the learned portion of human behavior, the learned part of the environment"; it is a way of life. The group of people that share a common culture is called a "society." All human beings share in common the same biological basis for culture. All cultures have similarities and differences. All cultures have a technology, an economic system, a social structure that includes the family and a system of social control as well as political organizations and government, an educational system, a belief system, a language system, a recreational or play system, and an aesthetic system.

Culture exhibits certain similarities in all societies because *homo sapiens* is one species, with the same psychological makeup, the same organic needs, and the same essential life experiences the world over. Yet, man has as many ways of satisfying the same organic and psychological needs as he has separate groups.

Cultural similarities may be summed up in terms of the content of the culture. All societies satisfy the same needs in many different ways. Why this immense variety in cultural behavior? Possible answers are that each group's culture is dictated by its biological heredity or by its geographic environment. Probably a better explanation may lie in the fact that man is highly flexible and adaptable and that he has lots of creative energy and intelligence left over after he has solved his basic problems of group life.

---

[3] David Bidney, *Theoretical Anthropology*, (New York: Columbia University Press, 1953), p. 24.

[4] John Biesanz and Mavis Biesanz, *Modern Society*, 2nd ed. (Englewood Cliffs, N. J.; Prentice-Hall, 1959).

Several other characteristics of culture are part of the definition: (a) Culture is socially transmitted—that is, learned from others. (b) Culture is ideational—carried in the minds of individual members of the society as a set of ideas, of common understandings about the right and proper thing to think, feel, say, and do in any given situation. (c) Culture is socially shared. (d) Culture can be preserved and accumulated; thus, it is highly stable and continuous. (e) Culture tends to be organized and integrated.

Society on the other hand, is primarily a concept of social structure, of social organization, and of group life and interaction. Among the basic elements of social structure are the institutions of the society, the social stratification system, and the social processes.

Problems in Disentangling the Culture and Society Concepts

In real life, then, cultural and social groups are so intertwined as to make it difficult to identify each element. This raises the question whether we are dealing with abstractions or with the way things are in real life.[5] We do this frequently in dealing with human behavior; for example, we speak about cognitive, affective, and psychomotor as abstractions. In flesh-and-blood terms all these elements are combined in the human being.

Finally, a very difficult problem arises from the fact that many Spanish-speaking people have been almost completely acculturated to the Anglo middle class while many others are still found at the traditional end of the acculturation scale. One gets the impression that those supporting the cultural difference hypothesis are really referring to those at the traditional culture end of the continuum and their ideas do not apply to those who to all intents and purposes have assimilated lower-class Anglo culture.

---

[5] There are a number of troublesome questions involved in this analysis. One relates to the fact that each culture has an economic system and that the social system has a stratification system and therefore a lower social class. One of the characteristics of the lower class is poverty, which under the culture-society categorization belongs in the culture category. Another relates to the problem whether one should conceive of culture as encompassing all social groups and whether there are then social class variations of the dominant culture. Finally, there is the conceptualization of the "culture of poverty" which incorporates elements of social class and culture.

I'm sure that many of you are thinking, as I am, that the attempt to disentangle these elements is an exercise in intellectualizing dear to the college professor. Why bother when one can take the totality of whatever Spanish-speaking problems there are, identify them specifically, and work toward their solution? If the teacher accepts the student and helps him to grow and develop, that is what is important. Let us approach children as children and not as children who are different because of color, culture, or social class position. All right then, let's quit talking about cultural differences.

Still, there is the nagging feeling that culture may be important. We observe the effects of culture at a gross level when we see that an American thinks, acts, moves, and feels differently from a Japanese in Japan or an Eskimo in Alaska or Canada. We know that perception is crucial in behavior and that culture effects perception. We know that culture tells us what to pay attention to, and what meaning to attach to what we see, and finally how we are to react. If it is this fundamental, surely, it must affect a student and must be taken into account in teaching and helping him learn.

Perhaps the most productive way to trace culture to behavior and eventually to teaching and learning is at the *feeling* rather than at the curricular or cognitive level. This would imply knowing how students *feel* about their families, their people, their food, their music, their art, themselves. It would imply empathizing with them as they go about their learning tasks in the school.

A rather prominent factor in the teaching/learning relationship which derives directly from the culture concept is that of *ethnocentrism.* This refers to the idea that *our* culture, *our* way of life, *our* way of doing things, *our* food, *our* customs are the best and that others are inferior. It is a universal phenomenon and an inevitable one. If carried to extreme forms it becomes a disadvantage, as for example, the teacher who feels that the WASP culture is the best and the Mexican-American, Indian, or Black culture is inferior. Teachers have reacted to ethnicity, color and other physical characteristics, torn or dirty clothing, and haircuts in stereotyped ways that have done much injustice to the students. These stereotypes are basically ethnocentric; they cannot be tolerated in teachers dealing with Spanish-speaking and Indian children.

I would like, finally, to attempt to apply some of the ideas to *learning.* We know that all children learn—that is, they modify their behavior. This means all are capable of learning. We know that all humans learn in basically the same way; that human intelligence develops in much the same way in all humans. Of late I have become interested in the work of Piaget and how to apply his concepts to help Spanish-speaking and Indian youngsters, and youngsters in general, develop their potential intelligence. What seems to happen with many students is that they fail to make the transition from concrete levels of thinking to the more abstract and formal levels of mature thought. It is vital here to discard the older concepts of intelligence that have done so much harm in classifying children as stupid and bright on the basis of intelligence tests and to substitute for them the notion that children come to us in school with certain resources developed to a certain level: our function is to pick them up at that point and help them develop. Part of what we have charged as a discriminatory middle-class curriculum, is, in fact, the continued application of psychological and educational concepts that no longer have any validity. Intelligence is one of these and the bias in favor of conceptual-verbal learning is another.

Recently there has been a great deal of interest in the notion of learning styles. The idea is that individuals have preferred modalities for learning. Everyone uses the senses for receiving data, but some may rely more upon one or more or particular combinations of senses in learning. Some of the ideas are reflected in the names given to these learning styles, such as "impulsive-reflective," "reception-discovery," "concrete-abstract." The question arises whether culture or social class conditions children to certain of these modalities. For example, the anthropologists have told us that communal cultures tend to be pragmatic, relating to the seen and experienced world rather than to an abstract one. One surmises that the thought processes used by communal people are related to the nonabstract. If so, the children of the people have been conditioned to nonabstract thought processes and perhaps to certain learning styles. This would, of course, place students conditioned by communal cultures at a distinct disadvantage in a school that emphasized conceptual verbal, that is abstract, thought processes. Perhaps also, this explains, in part, what happens in school to lower-class children whatever their cultural origins. The teaching task is to help students overcome the limitations of cultural or social conditioning so that they can progress in school.

Conclusions

Looking at the problem of the improvement of the lives of the Spanish-speaking, Indian, Negro, and lower-class peoples from a different point of view, it is apparent that economic factors loom large. The social distance between the advantaged majority and the disadvantaged minorities is great and with recent structural changes in American society is increasing instead of decreasing. This means that social rather than cultural factors are more important. Whether this is equally true in the pedagogical sphere is largely what this paper is all about.

It appears that both lower social class membership and culture have an impact on the Spanish-speaking and Indian students. The problem of the education of the state's minority groups is more than a purely linguistic one. To disentangle economic factors from cultural factors is an extremely difficult and complex task, due partly to the complexity of the culture concept itself and partly to the lack of sufficient knowledge derived from research regarding its impact on the teaching/learning processes. There has been over-simplification of the culture concept and failure to conceive of it as an integrated totality which includes cognitive, aesthetic, and evaluative elements. There has also been failure to take into account the great variability of acculturation that actually exists.

Additionally, from a pedagogical point of view, the insistence upon making culture the central variable channels thinking, and hence practice, away from much relevant experience derived from working with the disadvantaged which, at this stage of knowledge, might go further in improving the education of "culturally different" groups.

My own position at this time is that we should use culture and cultural differences as starting points, but if we stop there we miss the point of the real needs of the minority groups.

Many practical programs which are based on recognition of cultural differences should, of course, be continued; the language programs, the development and integration of Hispanic and Indian and Black cultural heritage materials into the curriculum, the "cultural awareness programs," to name only a few.

One of the most obvious, but extremely neglected, aspects of minority-group education is the improvement of intergroup relations between and among all minority groups and the majority groups. It will not be enough to have students and teachers learn more about each other's group contributions. Acceptance of each other begins with toleration, but this is a very low-level category in any kind of intergroup taxonomy. We badly need an intergroup taxonomy. We must get people to the stage of "feeling sensibility" and finally to the stage of working and living together without the obstacles of stereotyping, of scapegoating, of discrimination, and of hate that prevent common and effective human relations.

To my young teacher friend who naïvely thought that the question she asked me was easy to answer, I give thanks. I'm not sure that I can answer it even now, if I hold solely to cultural explanations. Finally, I hope that this paper is seen as a preliminary exploration which begins to open up new avenues of thought and practice. I am convinced, however, that if we cannot explain how we should teach minority group students differently from those of the majority group, we may do little actual good in the school. It seems to me that the use of cultural differences as a political tool, while perfectly justified, may be an obstacle in developing effective pedagogical practice. If so, let us be a little more careful in our differentiations lest in our zeal we hurt our bilingual children more than we help them.

Section Two

Bilingualism and Bilingual Education

5. Bilingualism and Education

A. Bruce Gaarder

Having one language at home and another at school means that pupils must be bilingual. Should schools encourage this? Numbers of studies have attempted to find evidence of the relationship between bilingualism and intelligence, but results have been contradictory. A fair summary would be that in many societies, bilinguals, especially if their first language is one of lower status, do much worse on intelligence tests than do monolingual speakers of the status language. But, argues Bruce Gaarder, the explanation is that these bilingual children have not been permitted to learn in their own language. Dr. Gaarder, a senior official in the U.S. Office of Education, has been closely involved with the implementation of the Bilingual Education Act, passage of which was assisted by his evidence before the Senate.

Mr. Chairman and members of the subcommittee, there were in 1960 about five million persons of school age (6–18) in the United States who had a non-English mother tongue. It is reliably estimated that over three million of this group did in fact retain the use of that tongue. In this group of school children who still use the non-English mother tongue, there are 1.75 million Spanish speakers, about 77,000 American Indians, and slightly over a million from some thirty additional language groups: French, German, Polish, Czech, Yiddish, Ukrainian, and many others. The situation is not known to have changed notably since 1960. These are the children we are concerned with, plus another million or so in the same category under six years of age and soon to enter the schools. They are necessarily and unavoidably bilingual children.

Prepared statement reprinted from the Report of the Special Subcommittee on Bilingual Education of the Committee on Labor and Public Welfare, United States Senate, Ninetieth Congress, 1967, pages 51–55, with the author's permission.

Bilingualism can be either a great asset or a great liability. In our schools millions of these youngsters have been cheated or damaged or both by well-intentioned but ill-informed educational policies which have made of their bilingualism an ugly disadvantage in their lives. The object of this testimony is to show the nature of the damage that has been done and suggest how it can be remedied in the future.

Bilingual education means the use of both English and another language—usually the child's mother tongue—as mediums of instruction in the schools. It is not "foreign language teaching" but rather the use of each language to teach all of the school curriculum (except, of course, the other language itself). There are five main reasons which support bilingual education. The first three apply to the child's years in the elementary school:

1. Children who enter school with less competence in English than monolingual English-speaking children will probably become retarded in their school work to the extent of their deficiency in English, if English is the sole medium of instruction. On the other hand, the bilingual child's conceptual development and acquisition of other experience and information could proceed at a normal rate if the mother tongue were used as an alternate medium of instruction. Retardation is not likely if there is only one or very few non-English-speaking children in an entire school. It is almost inevitable if the non-English language is spoken by large groups of children.

2. Non-English-speaking children come from non-English-speaking homes. The use of the child's mother tongue by some of the teachers and as a school language is necessary if there is to be a strong, mutually reinforcing relationship between the home and the school.

3. ·Language is the most important exteriorization or manifestation of the self, of the human personality. If the school, the all-powerful school, rejects the mother tongue of an entire group of children, it can be expected to affect seriously and adversely those children's concept of their parents, their homes, and of themselves.

The other two reasons apply when the bilingual child becomes an adult:

4. If he has not achieved reasonable literacy in his mother tongue—ability to read, write, and speak it accurately—it will be virtually useless to him for any technical or professional work where language matters. Thus, his unique potential career advantage, his bilingualism, will have been destroyed.

5. Our people's native competence in Spanish and French and Czech and all the other languages and the cultural heritage each language transmits are a national resource that we need badly and must conserve by every reasonable means.

I will return later to most of these points.

There is a vast body of writing by educators who believe that bilingualism is a handicap. The evidence seems at first glance to be obvious and incontrovertible. There is a clear, direct chain relationship between language competence, formal education, and economic status among Americans whose mother tongue is not English. The children speak Spanish, or Navajo, or French, and they do poorly in school: therefore, (so goes the argument) their bilingualism is to blame. Many researchers have established a decided correlation between bilingualism and low marks on intelligence tests, but what no research has shown is that bilingualism, per se, is a *cause* of low performance on intelligence tests. On the contrary, studies which have attempted to take into account all of the factors which enter the relationship show that it is not the fact of bilingualism but *how* and *to what extent* and *under what conditions* the two languages are taught that make the difference. (If this were not true, how could one explain the fact that the governing and intellectual elite in all countries have sought to give their children bilingual or even multilingual education?) Much of the literature on bilingualism does not deal at all with bilingual education. Rather it shows the unfortunate results when the child's mother tongue is ignored, deplored, or otherwise degraded.

The McGill University psychologists, Lambert and Peale (now Anisfeld) have shown that if the bilingualism is "balanced," i.e., if there has been something like equal, normal, literacy developed in the two languages, bilingual ten-year-olds in Montreal are markedly superior to monolinguals on verbal and nonverbal tests of intelligence and appear to have greater mental flexibility, a superiority in concept formation, and a more diversified set of mental abilities. It is their judgment that there is no evidence that the supposed "handicap" of bilingualism is *caused* by bilingualism, per se, and that "it would be more fruitful to seek that cause in the inadequacy of the measuring instrument and in other variables such as socioeconomic status, attitude toward the two languages, and educational policy and practice regarding the teaching of both languages."

There is an educational axiom, accepted virtually everywhere else in the world, that "the best medium for teaching a child is his mother tongue." What happens when the mother tongue is so used? A recent study made in Chiapas, Mexico, by Dr. N. Modiano for the New York University School of Education shows the results that can be expected. The Modiano research examined the hypothesis (implicit in current educational policies throughout the United States) that children of linguistic minorities learn to read English with greater comprehension when all reading instruction is offered through English than when they first learn to read in their non-English mother tongue.

The investigation involved all students attending twenty-six schools in three Indian *municipios* in Chiapas. All students were native speakers of either Tzeltal or Tzotzil, two of the indigeneous languages of Mexico. Thirteen were federal or state schools in which all reading instruction was offered in Spanish. Thirteen were National Indian Institute schools in which literacy was developed in the mother tongue prior to being attempted in Spanish. The purpose of the study was to determine which group of schools produced the greater measure of literacy (specifically, greater reading comprehension) in the national language, Spanish.

Two indications of reading comprehension were obtained. First, all teachers were asked to designate "all of your students who are able to understand what they read in Spanish." Approximately 20 percent of the students in the all-Spanish federal and state schools were nominated by their teachers as being able to understand what they were asked to read in Spanish. Approximately 37 percent of the students in the bilingual Institute schools were nominated by their teachers as being able to understand what they read in Spanish. This difference favors the bilingual approach beyond the .001 level of probability.

Then, a carefully devised group reading comprehension test was administered to all of the selected children. The children's average score in state and federal schools was 41.59; in the bilingual Institute schools it was 50.30. The difference between these means was found to be significant at beyond the .01 level of probability. Within each of the three *municipios* mean scores in Institute schools were higher than in federal and state schools. Thus, not only did the teachers using the bilingual approach nominate more of their students for testing, but their judgment was confirmed by the fact that their students scored significantly higher on the group test of reading comprehension.

In Puerto Rico, in 1925, the International Institute of Teachers College, Columbia University, made a study of the educational system on that island where English was the major medium of instruction despite the fact that the children's mother tongue is Spanish. The Columbia University group undertook a testing program to measure pupil achievement in all grades and particularly to explore the relative effectiveness of learning through each of the two language mediums. To test reading, arithmetic, information, language, and spelling they used the Stanford Achievement Test in its regular English version and in a Spanish version modified to fit Puerto Rican conditions. Over 69,000 tests were given.

The results were displayed on charts so as to reveal graphically any significant difference between achievement through English and achievement through Spanish. Both of these could be compared on the same charts with the average achievement of children in schools in the continental United States. I will summarize the findings in two sentences:

1. In comparison with children in the continental United States, the Puerto Ricans' achievement through English showed them to be markedly retarded.

2. The Puerto Rican children's achievement through Spanish was, by and large, markedly superior to that of continental United States children, who were using their own mother tongue, English.

The Columbia University researchers, explaining the astonishing fact that those elementary school children in Puerto Rico—poverty-stricken, backward, "benighted," beautiful Puerto Rico—achieved more through Spanish than continental United States children did through English, came to the following conclusion, one with extraordinary implications for us here:

Spanish is much more easily learned as a native language than in English.

The facility with which Spanish is learned makes possible the early introduction of content into the primary curriculum.

Every effort should be made to maintain it and to take the fullest advantage of it as a medium of school instruction.

What they were actually saying is that because Spanish has a much better writing system than English (i.e., the writing system matches the sound system) speakers of Spanish can master reading and writing very quickly and can begin to acquire information from the printed page more easily and at an earlier age.

The conclusion is, in sum, that if the Spanish-speaking children of our Southwest were given all of their schooling through both Spanish and English, there is a strong likelihood that not only would their so-called handicap of bilingualism disappear, but *they would have a decided advantage over their English-speaking schoolmates, at least in elementary school, because of the excellence of the Spanish writing system.* There are no "reading problems," as we know them, among school children in Spanish-speaking countries.

And their English could be better too, but that's another story.

American Samoa, with about 20,000 people, is an example of what it means when children, in communities which have a high degree of linguistic solidarity are required to study through a language not their own. In American Samoa the home language of the native people is Samoan, and they cling to it tenaciously, even to the extent of providing their children both after-school and weekend instruction in Samoan. In the villages there are also "pastor's schools" conducted in Samoan. In 1963 the Science Research Associates high school placement tests were given to 535 graduates of the Samoan junior high schools, i.e., pupils who had completed the ninth grade. The median grade placement score was 5.8, i.e., close to the end of the fifth grade. Only 21 of the 535 pupils scored 9.0, i.e., in the ninth grade, or better. Most of the 21 had studied in the United States or had other unusual advantages. The author of one report judged that one obstacle to the learning of English was the Samoans' pride in their own culture.

The most obvious anomaly—or absurdity—of our educational policy regarding foreign-language learning is the fact that we spend perhaps a billion dollars a year to teach the languages—in the schools, the colleges and universities, the Foreign Service Institute, the Department of Defense, AID, USIA, CIA, etc. (and to a large extent to adults who are too old ever to master a new tongue)—yet virtually no part of the effort goes to maintain and to develop the competence of American children who speak the same languages natively. There are over four million native speakers of French or Spanish in our country and these two languages are the two most widely taught, yet they are the ones for which our Government recognizes the greatest unfilled need (at the levels, for example, of the Foreign Service of the Department of State and the program of lecturers and technical specialists sent abroad under the Fulbright-Hays Act).

The establishment of bilingual education programs in our schools could be expected to increase and improve, rather than lessen, emphasis on the proper teaching of English to children who speak another mother tongue. Under our present policy, which supports the ethnocentric illusion that English is not a "foreign" language for anyone in this country, it is almost always taught as if the bilingual child already knew English. Our failure to recognize the mother tongue and thus to present English *as a second language* helps to produce "functional illiteracy" in almost three out of every four Spanish speakers in Texas.

In a bilingual education program, English would be taught from the child's first day in school but his concept development, his acquisition of information and experience—in sum, his total *education*—would not depend on his imperfect knowledge of English. Bilingual education permits making a clear distinction between education and language, i.e., between the content of education and the vehicle through which it is acquired.

I use the example of two window panes, the green-tinted Spanish one and the blue-tinted English one, both looking out on the same world, the same reality. We tell the little child who has just entered the first grade, "You have two windows into the world, the Spanish one and the English one. Unfortunately, your English window hasn't been built yet, but we're going to work on it as fast as we can and in a few years, maybe, it'll be as clear and bright as your Spanish window. Meantime, even if you don't see much, keep on trying to look out the space where the blue one will be. And stay away from the green one! It's against our educational policy to look through anything tinted green!"

The influx of Spanish-speaking Cuban refugee children into Florida in recent years brought about the establishment of two model bilingual education programs in the Dade County (Miami) public schools. The first is essentially a period a day of Spanish language arts instruction at all grade levels for native speakers of Spanish. It was established, according to educators there, "because it did not seem right not to do something to maintain and develop these children's native language." The second program is a model bilingual public elementary school (Coral Way) which is now finishing its fourth year of operation. This highly successful school provides us with information on three points of great importance in the present context:

1. At the fifth grade level the children have been found—insofar as this can be determined by achievement testing—to be able to learn equally well through either of their two languages. (This is a level of achievement that cannot be expected in even our best college-level foreign language programs.)

2. Since half of the children are Cubans and half begin as monolingual speakers of English, each learning the other's language and his own, it is apparent that a truly comprehensive bilingual education program can serve not only the non-English mother tongue children *who must necessarily become bilingual,* but also the ordinary monolingual American child who speaks nothing but English and *whose parents want him to become bilingual.*

3. The strength of the program lies in the high quality of the teachers of both languages (all of them native and highly trained speakers of the language in which they teach) and the fullness of the support they get from the school administration and the community. The implications of these three points are momentous.

RECOMMENDATIONS

1. That comprehensive programs of bilingual education in self-selected schools and for self-selected pupils at all school grade levels be supported.

2. That the opportunity to profit from bilingual education be extended to children of all non-English-speaking groups. All are now losers under our present educational one-language policy: at worst they become hopelessly retarded in school; at best they lose the advantage of mastery of their mother tongue.

3. That adequate provision be made for training and otherwise securing teachers capable of using the non-English tongue as a medium of instruction.

4. That there be provision for cooperative efforts by the public schools and the non-English ethnic organizations which have thus far worked unaided and unrecognized to maintain two-language competence in their children.

5. That provision be made for safeguarding the quality of the bilingual education programs which receive Federal financial assistance.

6. Bilingualism and Thought

John Macnamara

There are many situations in which bilinguals are members of a socially disadvantaged group—in much of the United States, "bilingual" is a euphemism for Mexican American. There is also good evidence that bilinguals suffer academically when they are forced to study in their weaker language, as John Macnamara has documented in his book *Bilingualism and Primary Education* (Edinburgh: Edinburgh University Press, 1966). The question remains, is there any inherent disadvantage in being a bilingual and learning two languages rather than one? In the paper that follows, Professor Macnamara, associate professor of psychology at McGill University, considers the evidence on the relationship between bilingualism and thought. It is one of many fine papers given at the 1970 Georgetown Round Table, which was devoted to bilingualism and language contact, as the 1969 Round Table had been to the teaching of English to speakers of other languages or dialects; the two reports, each edited by James Alatis, provide very readable and authoritative reviews of the state of the fields they cover.

If Whorf's hypothesis were true, if it were the case that differences among languages caused substantial differences in cognitive functioning, the bilingual person would be in a curious predicament. In his cognitive functioning, the bilingual would have to conform to one of three patterns, and each of the three would involve serious inconveniences. He might when using L_1 or L_2 always function cognitively in the manner appropriate to L_1 say; he would then have great difficulty in understanding speakers of L_2 or in being understood by them. Alternatively, he might always function cognitively in a manner appropriate to neither language and run the

Reprinted from the *Report of the Twenty-First Annual Round Table Meeting on Linguistics and Language Studies.* Ed. James Alatis (Washington, D.C.: Georgetown University Press, 1970), pp. 25-40, by permission of the author and the publishers.

risk of understanding or being understood by nobody. Or he might have two cognitive systems, one for each language. He could then communicate with speakers of either language but he would have great difficulty in "communicating" with himself. Whenever he switched languages he would have difficulty in explaining in L_2 what he had heard or said in L_1.

The implications which I am drawing from Whorf's hypothesis may seem preposterous, but I think that they follow logically. The differences in cognitive functioning which Whorf attributed to linguistic variables in syntax and vocabulary are far-reaching and profound. And though Whorf does not, to my knowledge, emphasize the effect which such differences might have on communication across language boundaries, the effects must surely be grave.

Our unwillingness to believe that the bilingual finds himself in the predicament I describe above is the measure of our unwillingness to accept the Whorfian hypothesis. But there are other grounds for caution. Psychologists, as Joshua Fishman (1960) points out, have been hard pressed to find any evidence in favor of the hypothesis. Only in its weakest form, only when it is taken as referring to the relationship between the suitability of vocabulary items to denote certain objects and some dependent cognitive functioning, is there support for Whorf in the psychological literature (see Lenneberg, 1967, and Miller and McNeill, 1969). Moreover, many of us instinctively join Church (1958) and Black (1959 and 1969) against Quine (1960) and numerous other philosophers in the view that one cannot establish a man's ontology from either his vocabulary or his grammar.

One is a little surprised, then, to hear Lounsbury (1969) say that in their thinking about limited areas of vocabulary and the related cognitive structures "the leading social anthropologists of today incline. . . in the direction of complete relativism" (Lounsbury, 1969: 14). Lounsbury is referring specifically to kinship systems, but his remarks can presumably be extended to cover other folk taxonomies. The root reason for the prevailing opinion is the hope, perhaps even the belief, that the componential analysis of folk taxonomies reveals psychological entities. Indeed several of the leading exponents of the art, Goodenough (1956), Frake (1962), Mathiot (1969), and Wallace (1962) have made statements which suggest that they are laying bare the bases used by people in classifying their environment. On the other hand, it is only fair to point out that this belief has been seriously questioned several times by social anthropologists themselves; see, for example, Burling (1969), Hymes (1969), Lounsbury (1969), and Wallace (1965). The claim that componential analysis reveals psychologically valid entities runs into Burling's (1969) objection that any set of terms can be analyzed, or systematically divided, in several different ways. Since each division demands a set of components somewhat different from any other division, and since the choice of one division rather than another is arbitrary, it follows that the psychological validity of the resultant components is highly questionable. Moreover, as Vermazen (1967) observes in discussing a similar problem connected with Katz and Fodor's (1963) model of lexical structure, there is no principled way of selecting components or bases of classification. We can effectively distinguish men from women, for example, on the basis of skin texture, body outline, length of finger nails, hair ribbons, and the like without ever needing to carry the study further. The seemingly obvious candidate for component status, then, need not be the one which people generally employ. The truth is that we know very little about the bases which people use for classifying the most familiar objects in their environment (see Polanyi, 1968), and it is unlikely that language on its own should provide the answer.

The point of all this is to emphasize once again the lesson which psychologists drew from their studies of Whorf's hypothesis. Linguistic evidence on its own can be used to support linguistic conclusions only, never psychological ones. Since anthropologists have seldom gone beyond linguistic evidence in their analyses of folk taxonomies, it would be premature to make claims of psychological validity for their componential systems. It follows, too, that one would be unwise to base claims for Whorfian relativism on such analyses.

Coordinate-compound distinction

The coordinate-compound distinction to which I now want to turn is closely related to Whorfian relativism. Indeed I hope to show that in some of its forms it is a veiled version of such relativism. It was mainly Uriel Weinreich (1953) in his book, *Languages in Contact,* who drew the attention of psychologists to the distinction.

In that book he tentatively suggests that on semantic grounds bilinguals seem to fall into three types, which I shall call by the names which have subsequently become stándard. "Coordinate" bilinguals are those for whom the corresponding pair of terms in two languages signify two distinct semantemes. "Compound" bilinguals are those for whom corresponding terms signify a single semanteme. "Subordinate" bilinguals are those for whom a term in L_2 signifies first a term in L_1 and signifies a semanteme only indirectly. The three types may be illustrated by means of Weinreich's own diagrams in which he uses the Russian word *kniga* "book" together with the English word *book*.

(1) Coordinate　　　(2) Compound　　　(3) Subordinate

'book'　'kníga'　　　'book'　'kníga'　　$\left\{ \begin{array}{c} \text{'book'} \\ \hline \text{/buk/} \end{array} \right\}$
　|　　　|　　　　　　|　　　|　　　　　　　　|
/buk/　/kn iga/　　/buk/　/kn iga/　　　　　/kn iga/

In Ervin and Osgood (1954) the subordinate type is subsumed into the compound one and criteria are given for judging to which of the two remaining types a bilingual belongs. Compounds are those who either learned one language through the medium of the other, as in old-fashioned language classes, or learned both languages in the same context, the home for instance. The coordinates or "true" bilinguals are those who learned the two languages in different contexts, such as L_1 at home and L_2 at school (presumably by the direct method) and at work. Ervin and Osgood's illustration of the two types are shown in Figure 1 in which S and R stand for sign and response respectively,

Figure 1.

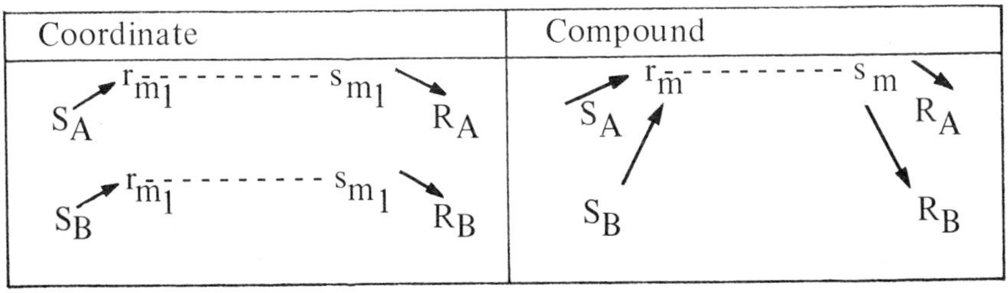

r and *s* stand for "mediating processes or meanings," and the subscripts *A* and *B* stand for different languages as do the subsubscripts 1 and 2 in the diagram for coordinates. Not wishing to start old battles all over again, I will rest content with two observations about this theory. It falls heir to all the criticism that Chomsky (1959), Fodor (1965), and others have made of *S-R* attempts to handle the phenomena of language. In addition, and here I am sure its authors would agree today, it is quite inadequate as a representation of the lexical structure which must be employed by anyone who speaks a natural language. Space permits me to do little more than refer to a number of sources: Chomsky (1965), Katz (1966), Katz and Fodor (1963), Katz and Postal (1964), Macnamara (in press), Macnamara and O'Clérigh (1969), Quillian (1967 and 1968), and Weinreich (1966). Among the principal weaknesses of the Ervin and Osgood model is the fact that it makes no provision for denotation as distinct from connotation or for emotive meaning as distinct from either. Moreover the model does not discuss the problem of selecting an appropriate meaning from among the many meanings of a polysemous term, although this is one of the major criteria which a satisfactory semantic theory must meet.

I fear that the man whose lead I have long followed in the study of bilingualism has added somewhat to the confusion which surrounds the coordinate-compound distinction. In some recent papers (Lambert, 1966; Lambert and Rawlings, 1969; Segalowitz and Lambert, 1969) he shifts the distinction between coordinate and compound bilingualism to one between early and late bilingualism. Compound bilinguals are those who acquire both languages in their homes before they go to school; coordinate bilinguals are those who began to acquire their second language after school age. In this new way of classifying bilinguals he is joined by Stafford (1968) and by Stafford and Van Keuren (1968).

But to return to the point of departure! Through all the variations in the interpretation of the terms, "coordinate" and "compound," the distinction has always been a semantic one and for Ervin and Osgood, unless I am mistaken, it was a Whorfian one. Ervin and Osgood's compound bilinguals had a single set of "representational mediation processes" for the two languages, whereas their coordinates had two sets of such processes, one for each language. Since mediation processes in their system are *caused* by signs or stimuli, it is fair to say that differences between languages cause different cognitive, nonlinguistic, mediating processes. For example, French uses the word *couper* in connection with the cutting of hair with a scissors and also the cutting up of a joint of meat with a knife; standard English divides the function of *couper* between *cut* and *carve* respectively. It follows that a coordinate French-English bilingual could well have different mediating processes associated with *couper* and *cut*. Admittedly, Ervin and Osgood seek to avoid the resultant inconveniences by suggesting that across languages the differences between translation equivalents are mostly slight. But as the above example shows this is not true. Ervin and Osgood also permit of elaborate connections between the coordinate's parallel mediating processes, in order to account for translation. Such connections might seem at first to preclude the plight of the Whorfian bilingual who cannot communicate with himself, who when he switches to L_2 can never make out what he has heard or said in L_1. But Ervin and Osgood's additional associations will not preclude this difficulty; they are not equivalent to an instruction "compare and contrast," and make good any differences discovered by having recourse to other linguistic materials and other mediation processes. Yet only by means of such an instruction and a device to operate it could a person with something like "coordinate systems" ever switch languages without becoming hopelessly lost.

Lest you think that I am being unfair to the Ervin and Osgood model, permit me to point out two other related difficulties. The model has no system which would permit of two sets of mediating processes associated with a single term and for permitting context to select between them. Yet the cutting of hair with a scissors and the carving of meat with a knife might well give rise to distinct mediation processes which might well compete for possession of a Frenchman's head when *couper* was encountered. Furthermore, Osgood's semantic system, like all the other ones which have since been proposed, does not handle grammar. Apart from anything else, this means the model is confined to pairs of lexical items; hence it cannot guard against the inconveniences I have outlined by systematically relating *viande couper* in one expression and *cheveux* with *couper* in another expression so as to ensure that only the appropriate mediating processes are elicited.

On the subject of research into the coordinate-compound distinction I have little to add to what I wrote in the *Journal of Social Issues* in 1967. I then considered the evidence for the distinction to be exiguous, and I have seen no reason since to change my mind. I agree with Diller (1967) that the distinction as it stands is most likely a "conceptual artifact," and I am fearful for the sturdiness of the tall cognitive and personality structures which Diebold (1968) builds upon it. Perhaps my basic trouble is my belief that nothing like an adequate semantic system has been worked out for any language, let alone related semantic systems for two languages in bilingual harness.

This need not mean that we abandon work on the semantic systems of bilinguals; it is rather an invitation *reculer pour mieux sauter.* I suspect that the original inspiration for the coordinate-compound distinction owes more to instances of semantic interference than to Whorfian relativism. This sort of interference is well known; it is beautifully illustrated for example by Professor Mackey (1962 and 1965). For instance, the Irish word *lámh* is the nearest equivalent to the English word *hand* in the sense of human member. However, unlike *hand, lámh* includes "arm" in its denotation. If we start out not from words but from semantic fields we find numerous situations which I have previously illustrated with the French word *couper* serving the function of the English words *cut* and *carve* in at least some of their senses. It seems to me that such differences between the semantic systems of languages might well give rise to a whole range of bilinguals who vary in the extent to which they keep the semantic systems of their two languages distinct. Furthermore, I agree with Kolers (1963) and Fishman (1964) that the manner in which a person has learned his languages is unlikely to fix his semantic systems for life. Some may start out with fused semantic systems and gradually sort them out; others may start out with separate systems but gradually permit them to merge. Indeed, as John Gumperz (1964) has pointed out, it may be that distinct semantic systems can be maintained only by a person who makes a great conscious effort to do so, and much good language teaching is aimed precisely at achieving this effect.

At this point I want to forestall a possible source of confusion. The sort of distinction between semantic systems of which I have been speaking does not at all suggest a Whorfian relativism. It does not suggest that an Englishman either carves meat differently from a Frenchman, or perceives the carving of meat differently from a Frenchman, or is the least different from a Frenchman in his approach to meat, simply because as an Englishman he has a special term for the action of slicing meat with a knife. Neither is there any suggestion that an Irishman's knowledge of anatomy is more confused than that of an Englishman. All I want to suggest is that when a well-educated Irish-English bilingual cashes the terms in the two languages, he may get different semantic values for the words *lámh* and *hand*; a bilingual who does not know the languages so thoroughly is likely to get the same value for both words, even when he should not. It follows that when the well-educated bilingual needs to denote precisely that which the word *hand* denotes, he has to go beyond the word *lámh* and either add a modifying expression or choose a different lexical item.

It may help to be more precise about the advantages of employing a distinction based on degree of semantic interference rather than the coordinate-compound distinction. The first is clarity. Any clarity which the coordinate-compound distinction seemed to have was deceptive. Weinreich said the *kniga* and *book* might denote different "semantemes" for a coordinate bilingual, but he did not clarify what he meant by a "semanteme" or how the two semantemes related to these words might differ. The differences between Ervin and Osgood's coordinates and compounds are securely locked inside the head where no one can see them. In contrast, I am tying semantic interference to denotation and more specifically what I might call "denotational extent." In the limited illustrative materials which I have used, *lámh* has a wider denotational extension than *hand* and *cut* has a narrower denotational extension than *couper.* At a less concrete level, *conscience* (French) has a wider denotational extension than *conscience* (English).

Admittedly, I am not proposing any formal model of information processing or language processing, but then I do not believe that formalism in these areas is profitable at the present time. Formalism often results in hardening of the intellectual arteries; I for one feel freer working from a nonformal base to explore the broad strategies of semantic functioning. One such strategy must call for an ability to relate the incoming linguistic message to stored information and to systems which process such information. Quillian (1968) points out that a highly likely sense for an ambiguous symbol can frequently be determined simply on the basis of frequency of association. For instance, frequency suggests the meaning "down tools" for *strike* in (1) though other meanings are possible.

(1) The foreman called a strike.

The problem discussed by Bar-Hillel (1964: 174–79) is rather different. He noted that the meaning "enclosure in which children play" is determined for *pen* in (2) on the basis of the relative sizes of boxes and pens in the sense of "writing instruments."

(2) The box is in the pen.

The successful interpretation of the word *pen* in (2), then, depends on access to stored information at the moment of recall. This follows from the fact that few will have readily available as a piece of information the fact that boxes are rarely small enough to fit inside even a large writing pen. Since we could presumably use the relative sizes of writing pens and any other physical objects with which we are familiar, it is more parsimonious to hypothesize a function which permits us to compare sizes, whenever such information is required, than to store the results of innumerable comparisons. On the assumption that this is correct, I would suggest further that such information is for the most part stored and processed nonlinguistically and probably unconsciously.

Ulric Neisser (1967) has recently made an excellent case for the theory of analysis by synthesis in perception. In essence, the theory proposes that on the basis of partial information one can usually form a correct hypothesis about that which one is perceiving. Applied to language this means that on the basis of partial information, linguistic, nonlinguistic, and stochastic, one can usually form a correct hypothesis about that which someone is trying to communicate. One of course tests the hypothesis against further information which comes one's way and if necessary modifies the hypothesis. My reason for mentioning the theory here is to suggest that if it is correct in broad outline—and it seems to be—we must visualize the human language user as a far more dynamic agent in his approach to speech than either Whorf or bilingual theory builders seem to imagine. More-over, it seems likely that linguistic processes are only a small part of the cognitive functioning which is associated with either the produc-tion or the interpretation of speech. Furthermore, this very dyna-mism is surely the reason that the bilingual does not end up in any of the impasses to which Whorfian theorizing and the Ervin and Osgood model of coordinate and compound bilingualism seem inevitably to lead.

Bilingualism and IQ

The issues of which I have been speaking raise other more far-reaching issues which unfortunately I can do little more than allude to in this paper. The suggestion that linguistic functioning is to a great extent dependent on nonlinguistic functioning of many sorts is bound to disturb many philosophical spirits. However, it ties in nice-ly with the theory of Vygotsky (1962) and the oft-repeated theory of Piaget (see, for example, 1963 and 1965) that the origin of thought is distinct from that of language, and that insofar as the two are related in the early stages, language is the dependent partner. The investigations of Piaget's student, Sinclair-de-Zwart (1967 and 1969) support this theory and suggest that even in school children the development of basis cognitive schemata owe little to language, but rather that developments in language which occur at this time are dependent on prior nonlinguistic growth.

Essentially in the same tradition are recent papers by Bever (1970), Hebb, Lambert, and Tucker (1970), and Macnamara (1970) all arguing for a much closer integration of nonlinguistic cognitive functioning with linguistic functioning than has been common in most of the recent discussions of language acquisition. In my paper, I attempt to establish the thesis that the majority of linguistic univers-als are due to certain essential features of human intelligence. These are the features which ensure that mathematics, logic and science are essentially the same the world over; these are the reason that every language is translatable into every other language; these are the basic reasons for disbelieving Whorf.

Such communality in human intelligence has been obscured by the development of psychometrics and by the accompanying emphasis in psychology on individual differences. From their earliest beginnings intelligence tests have been designed to reveal individual differences in intelligence; they have never been designed for the purpose of revealing the essentials of intelligence. No analysis of IQs, then, however sophisticated or however comprehensive, could ever reveal what intelligence is; so it is little wonder that psychometric discussions on the topic have been barren. I suspect that the results of concentrating on IQs and on individual differences have been even more baneful than fruitless discussion of the nature of intelligence; I suspect that they have drawn attention away from factors which contribute to the development of intelligence. If I may be permitted to point a moral, one notices how interesting studies of child language became when in the early 1960's scholars abandoned the individual differences approach of earlier years and focussed instead upon the essentials of the process in which children differ very little. A similar moral can be drawn from the experimentally feeble and statistically naïve investigations of Jean Piaget, which have yielded results of interest which have been replicable the world over.

This is the background against which I would like to pose the question so often posed by students of bilingualism, does bilingualism affect intelligence? Against such a background one wonders what the question might mean. I have never seen the question discussed in this context, but it seems unlikely that bilingualism should have any effect upon the development of the basic, common, cognitive structures. The question, however, has usually been translated into the form, does bilingualism affect IQ? In that form it is almost trivial. An indefinitely large number of factors can affect IQ without having any *direct* bearing on what we intuitively recognize as intelligence. Among such factors is command of language. Under certain circumstances bilingual children have frequently been found to have a poorer command of their school language than their unilingual counterparts—see Macnamara (1966). Under similar circumstances bilinguals have generally scored a lower mean verbal IQ than unilinguals, but not a lower mean nonverbal IQ—see Darcy (1953 and 1963). It seems then that grasp of the language variety in which an IQ test is couched can affect the outcome of the test—an honest but hardly a surprising discovery.

What does all this amount to? Instinctively I want to say that the results just mentioned do not mean that bilinguals are more stupid than unilinguals, they have only been made to appear so. I well realize, however, that deficiencies in the standard version of a school language can constitute added difficulty in schoolwork. Tom Kellaghan and John Macnamara (1967) have shown that such difficulties can arise from something other than ignorance of certain words, idioms, and syntactic structures; they can arise from a fairly generalized unfamiliarity with and poor control of the standard language, at least in written form, so as to affect a student's problem-solving ability adversely. To conclude, then, bilinguals probably have need of some special help with language; poor control of the school language could well prevent a child from developing competence in several important areas of schoolwork. Granted that difficulties with the language are overcome, however, there is no reason to believe that bilingualism of itself should affect school progress in any way, adversely or beneficially. But of course a second language usually means access to a whole new world of people, literature, and ideas, and so bilingualism can be an enormous advantage.

Before passing on to the last section, it is worth pausing for a moment to consider where the study of bilingualism and IQ fits in with Whorfian relativism and the coordinate-compound distinction. There is probably no direct connection between them; nevertheless they are all related to some more general view of the connection between language and thought. The fears, or hopes, which caused people to study the relationship between bilingualism and IQ seem to spring from the general view that language either constitutes or creates intelligence. It is not difficult to see how such a view is related to Whorfian relativism and to the Ervin and Osgood models for coordinates and compounds. It follows then, that the basic objections to both Whorfian relativism and the Ervin and Osgood semantic models can also be used against a direct causal connection which would make intelligence dependent upon bilingualism.

Bilingualism and creativity

The whole study of creativity which has waxed and waned over the past ten years seems to be bedeviled to an even greater degree than the study of intelligence. The enterprise to explain creativity in school children has had two main objectives: (1) to prove that something could be measured which was largely independent of IQ; (2) to purify measures of this "something" and use them to establish a range of individual differences in it (see Dacey and Madaus, 1969). Very little attention indeed has been paid to this "something" or to the notion of creativity or to the relationship between creativity and intelligence. The fact that measures of creativity were designed almost entirely for the purpose of revealing individual differences in creativity meant that they were bound to miss the essentials of creativity, just as IQs miss the essentials of intelligence. The requirement that IQs and measures of creativity should as far as possible be orthogonal meant that the whole enterprise was committed from the outset to the trivial task of establishing that intelligence and creativity can differ in some peripheral ways. It is hardly unfair to say that the enterprise has been barren.

The whole thrust of Jean Piaget's life work has been to show that intelligence is essentially creative. If anything, he has attributed too much creativity to the mind and failed to stress the fact that the neonate must have a great deal of mental structure to explain intellectual creativity. Be that as it may, however, the main point is that the most important body of investigation into the nature of human intelligence results in the conclusion that the mind is essentially creative—hardly a happy augury for studies of creativity which start from the assumption that the two are different in kind. To Piaget's work may be added the body of theoretical and empirical work on language which clusters around the writings of Noam Chomsky. Chomsky stresses the creativity involved in the use of natural language and others (see, for example, McNeill, 1966) have found that the process of learning a language is a creative one. Perhaps the study of creativity would not have been so fruitless if it had been appreciated from the start that what its investigators were hunting for was not creativity at all, but rather unusual creations. That would not have given the investigators any greater guarantee of validity for their measures, but it would have set them free of the constraint that sought to justify the notion of creativity by showing that it could be distinguished from IQ.

Students of bilingualism have also wondered about the possibility that bilingualism should make people more creative. As I imagine Professor Lambert will discuss the evidence later in the conference, I will be brief. Both he and I are cautious about claims that bilingualism "generates" creativity, though he tends to be more optimistic than I do. Apart altogether from the theoretical considerations which I mentioned, I am not impressed by the evidence that has been produced to indicate that bilinguals tend to be more creative than monolinguals. Taking the theoretical considerations into account, in particular the total absence of any indications of validity for measures of creativity in school children, I am of the opinion that the topic of bilingualism and creativity comes under Wittgenstein's rubric: *woven man nicht reden kann, darüber muss man schweigen.*

Conclusion: Wanted—a theory of semantics

The saying that it is part of wisdom not to know (*ignorare*) certain things is attributed to Erasmus. I am not sure that I know what it means, but I would like it to include a counsel to realize and admit when we do not know something. Most of the topics which I have discussed have led me to make negative statements: I do not believe that there is any evidence to justify claims of Whorfian relativism; I do not believe that there is any evidence that there are two different sorts of bilinguals, coordinate and compound, at least as these have been described in the literature; I do not believe that bilingualism is directly related to intelligence; I do not believe that bilingualism is directly related to creativity. I want to add one other disclaimer to these: I am not even sure that the pair of concepts which are dissociated in each of these four statements are essentially unrelated. In other words, I am not even sure that any negativism is justified.

The reason is that each section of this paper is about the relationship between language and some aspect of thought and we have no semantic theory which even remotely approaches adequacy. Furthermore, I am not at all convinced that the empirical investigations to which I have alluded in this paper have contributed much to the building up of such a theory. Yet without an adequate theory of semantics, psychology, and linguistics (and possibly philosophy), we rapidly reach an impasse. One has the impression of one vogue succeeding another without any substantial progress. For what it is worth, my feeling is that valuable insights are going to come only through careful studies of infants, the development of their psychological functioning as a whole, of their classification of objects and the bases of such classification, of the assumptions which they make or do not make in their approaches to the world about them and in their approaches to language, of their ability to generalize, and the like. Furthermore, we need more careful studies of how language learning relates to other psychological developments. Among such studies, the analysis of bilingual language learning will have an honorable position. The road will be longer and more arduous, I imagine, than that which led to the major discoveries of modern physics, but the rewards will, I hope, be greater and less pregnant with destructive power.

REFERENCES

Bar-Hillel, Joshua. *Language and Information.* Reading Mass.: Addison-Wesley, 1964.

Bever, T. G. "The Cognitive Basis for Linguistic Structures," in *Cognition and Language Learning,* ed. J. R. Hayes. New York: Wiley, 1970.

Black, Max. "Linguistic Relativity: The Views of Benjamin Lee Whorf." *Philosophical Review,* 68 (1959), 228–38.

———. "Some troubles with Whorfianism." *Language and Philosophy: A Symposium,* ed. Sidney Hook. New York: New York University Press, 1969, 30–35.

Burling, Robbins. 1969. 30–35. "Cognition and Componential Analysis: God's Truth or Hocus-pocus?" *Cognitive Anthropology,* ed. Stephen A. Tyler. New York: Holt, 1969, 419–28.

Chomsky, Noam. Review of B. F. Skinner: *Verbal Behavior* Language, 35 (1959), 26–58.

———. *Aspects of the Theory of Syntax.* Cambridge, Mass.: M.I.T. Press, 1965.

Church, A. "Ontological commitment." *Journal of Philosophy,* 55 (1958), 1008–14.

Dacey, John S. and George F. Madaus. "Creativity: Definitions, Explanations and Facilitation." Irish Journal of Education, 3 (1969), 55–69.

Darcy, Natalie T. "A review of the Literature on the Effects of Bilingualism upon the Measurement of Intelligence." *Journal of Genetic Psychology,* 82 (1953), 21–58.

———. "Bilingualism and the Measurement of Intelligence: Review of a Decade of Research." *Journal of Genetic Psychology,* 103 (1963), 259–82.

Diebold, Richard A. "The Consequences of Early Bilingualism in Cognitive Development and Personality Formation." *The study of personality: An Interdisciplinary Appraisal.* Ed. E. Norbeck, D. Price-Williams, and W. M. McCord. New York: 1968, 218–45.

Diller, Karl C. "'Compound' and 'Coordinate' Bilingualism—a Conceptual Artifact." Paper presented to the Linguistic Society of America, Chicago, Illinois (mimeo), 1967.

Ervin, Susan, and Charles E. Osgood, "Second Language Learning and Bilingualism." *Journal of Abnormal and Social Psychology.* (Supplement), 49 (1954), 139–46.

Fishman, Joshua A. "A Systematization of the Whorfian Hypothesis." Behav-

ioral Science, 5 (1960), 232–39.
———. "Language maintenance and language shift as a field of inquiry." *Linguistics*, 9 (1964), 32–70.
Fodor, Jerry A. "Could Meaning Be an r_m?" *Journal of Verbal Learning and Verbal Behavior*, 4 (1965), 74–81.
Frake, Charles O. "The Ethnographic Study of Cognitive Systems." *Anthropology and Human Behavior*. Ed. Thomas Gladwin and William C. Sturtevant, Washington, D.C.: Anthropological Society of Washington, 1962.
Goodenough, Ward H. "Componential Analysis and the Study of Meaning." *Language*, 32 (1956), 195-216.
Gumperz, John J. "Linguistic and Social Interaction in Two Communities." *The Ethnography of Communication*. Ed. John J. Gumperz and Dell H. Hymes. American Anthropologist, Special Publication 3 (1964), 137–53.
Hebb, Donald O., Wallace E. Lambert, and G. Richard Tucker. "Language, Thought and Experience." McGill University, Department of Psychology, (mimeo) (1970).
Hymes, Dell H. "Discussion of Burling's paper." *Cognitive Anthropology*. Ed. Stephen A. Tyler. New York: Holt, 1969.
Katz, Jerrold J. *The Philosophy of Language*. New York: Harper Row, 1966.
———, and Jerry A. Fodor. *"The Structure of Semantic Theory."* Language 39 (1963), 170–210.
———, and Paul M. Postal. *An Integrated Theory of Linguistic Description*. Cambridge, Mass.: M.I.T. Press, 1964.
Kellaghan, Thomas, and John Macnamara. "Reading in a Second Language." *Reading Instruction: An International Forum*. ed. Marion D. Jenkinson. Newark, Del.: International Reading Association, 1967, 231–40.
Kolers, Paul A. "Interlingual Word Associations." *Journal of Verbal Learning and Verbal Behaviour*. 2 (1963), 291–300.
Lambert, Wallace E. "Psychological Studies of the Interdependencies of the Bilinguals Two Languages." *Substance and Structure in Language*. Ed. Jaan Puhvel. University of California Press, 1969, 99–126.
———, and Chris Rawlings. "Bilingual Processing of Mixed-Language Associative Networks." *Journal of Verbal Learning and Verbal Behaviour*, 8 (1969), 604–09.
Lenneberg, Eric H. *Biological Foundations of Language*. New York: Wiley, 1967.
Lounsbury, Floyd G. "Language and Culture." *Language and Philosophy: A Symposium*. Ed. Sidney Hook. New York: New York University Press, 1969, 3–29.
Mackey, William F. "The Description of Bilingualism." Canadian Journal of Linguistics, 7 (1962), 51–85.
———. "Bilingual Interference: Its Analysis and Measurement." *Journal of Communication*, 15 (1965), 239–49.
Macnamara, John. *Bilingualism and Primary Education*. Edinburgh: Edinburgh University Press, 1966.
———. "The Bilingual's Linguistic Performance—A Psychological Overview." Journal of Social Issues, 23 (1967), 58–77.
——— "The Cognitive Basis of Language Learning in Infants." Montreal Department of Psychology. McGill University, (mimeo) (1970).

————. "Parsimony and the Lexicon." *Language.* In press.
————, and Anne O. Cléirigh. "Studies in the Psychology of Semantics: The Projection Rules." Dublin: Educational Research Center, St. Patrick's College, (mimeo) (1969).
Mathiot, Madelaine. "The Semantic and Cognitive Domain of Language." University of California, Los Angeles, (mimeo) (1969).
McNeill, David. "The Creation of Language by Children." *Psycholinguistic papers: The Proceedings of the 1966 Edinburgh Conference.* Ed: John Lyons and Roger J. Wales. Edinburgh: Edinburgh University Press, 1966, 99–115.
Miller, George A., and David McNeill. "Psycholinguistics." *Handbook of Social Psychology.* Ed. G. Lindzey and E. Aronson. Reading, Mass.: Addison-Wesley, 1969.
Neisser, Ulric. *Cognitive Psychology.* New York: Appleton-Century-Crofts, 1967.
Piaget, Jean. "Langage et operations intellectuelles." In *Problèmes de psycholinguistique. Symposium de l'association de psychologie scientifique de langue française.* Paris: Presses Universitaires de France, 1963.
————. *La formation du symbole chez l'enfant: imitation, jeu et rêve, image et représentation.* 3rd ed.: Neuchatel, Delachaux, et Niestlé, 1965.
Polanyi, Michael. "Logic and Psychology." *American Psychologist,* 3 (1968), 27–43.
Quillian, M. Ross. "Word Concepts: A Theory Simulation of Some Basic Semantic Capabilities." *Behavioral Science.* 12 (1967), 410–30.
————. "Semantic Memory." *Semantic Information Processing.* Ed. Marvin Minsky. Cambridge, Mass.: M.I.T. Press, 1968, 216–70.
Quine, Willard Van Orman. *Word and Object.* New York: Wiley, 1960.
Segalowitz, Norman, and Wallace E. Lambert. "Semantic generalization in Bilinguals." *Journal of Verbal Learning and Verbal Behaviour.* 8 (1969), 559–66.
Sinclair-de-Zwart, Hermina. *Acquisition de langage et développement de la pensée.* Paris: Dunad, 1967.
————. "Developmental Psycholinguistics." *Studies in Cognitive Development: Essays in Honor of Jean Piaget.* Ed. David Elkind and John H. Flavell. New York: Oxford University Press, 1969, 315–36.
Stafford, Kenneth R. "Problem solving as a function of language." *Language and Speech,* 11 (1968), 104–12.
————, and Stanley R. Van Kauren. "Semantic Differential Profiles as Related to Monolingual–Bilingual Types." *Language and Speech.* 11 (1968), 167–70.
Vermazen, Bruce. Review of *An Integrated Theory of Linguistic Descriptions* by J. J. Katz and P. M. Postal, and *The Philosophy of Language* by J. J. Katz. *Synthese,* 17 (1967), 35–365.
Vygotsky, Lev S. *Thought and Language.* Cambridge, Mass.: M.I.T. Press, 1962.
Wallace, Anthony F. C. "Culture and Cognition." *Science,* 135 (1962), 351–57.
————. "The Problem of the Psychological Validity of Componential Analysis." *Formal Semantic Analysis,* Ed. E.A. Hammel, Menasha, Wis.: American Anthropological Association, 1965, 229–48.
Weinreich, Uriel. Languages in contact. Publications of the Linguistic Circle, No. 1. New York, 1953.
————. "Explorations in Semantic Theory." *Current Trends in Linguistics.* Ed. Thomas A. Sebeok. vol. 3. The Hague, Mouton: 1966, III, 395–477.

7. Bilingualism as a Social Force

Ralph W. Yarborough

The term "bilingual education" was seldom heard in the United States before 1967, but then there was a sudden burst of activity throughout the country, focused on the efforts to pass the Bilingual Education Act. One of its strongest proponents was the Honorable Ralph W. Yarborough, Democratic Senator from the state of Texas, and his work in large measure contributed to the passing of Title VII, Bilingual Education Program, of the Elementary and Secondary Education Act. In December 1968, Senator Yarborough gave the following address to the joint conventions of the Modern Language Association and the American Council on the Teaching of Foreign Languages.

This is not going to be a scholarly presentation; it is not meant to be. Although United States Senators are said to have the rhetorical gifts required to sell refrigerators to Eskimos, monolingual Senators have not been accused of making pretensions of scholarship in the field of bilingualism at a meeting of eminent bilingual scholars.

Rather, what I intend to do is share some of my thinking with you toward the end of providing a better life for Americans—in the hope that you will apply your scholarship and your knowledge and your experience to offer advice on appropriate courses of action.

In my endeavors with the Bilingual Education Act of 1967, I received considerable assistance from many of you; and for that reason, I think the Bilingual Education Act is destined for success. It

Reprinted from *Foreign Language Annals,* 2, 1969, pages 325–57, by permission of the author and publishers.

was drafted, fought for, and passed because of a crying need among the three million school-age American children who come from non-English-speaking homes. To implement the Act, the first applications for grants are just beginning to come into the Office of Education, so it is too early to report on what is going to happen under the Act, but it is *not* too early to plan further for the future.

Perhaps the most important single item that needs attention in the field of bilingual education is funding; money, plain and simple. The Congress authorized the expenditure, during fiscal 1968, of $15 million, but not one red cent was appropriated. The Congress authorized funding during fiscal 1969 of $30 million for the Bilingual Education Act; the Administration recommended a funding level of only $5 million; the House of Representatives on a 96-95 vote decided against any funding whatsoever. When the appropriations bill came over to the Senate, an appropriation of $10 million was obtained. In conference with the House that amount was compromised to the present figure of $7.5 million.

You know, and I know, that $7.5 million is nothing but token-ism—that even if the full $30 million had been appropriated, it would make only a dent, but a very significant dent, in the problems faced by those more than three million children who are bruised and battered as they confront the language barrier. And so we need to work to get full funding this next year—$45 million—for bilingual education. That takes work; work by me and work by you. Members of Congress who make the decision about money need convincing by experts like you that money needs to be appropriated and expended for bilingual education. For these three million school children, if there is no bilingual education, there is little education of any sort.

Before suggesting possible amendments to the Bilingual Education Act itself, let us discuss another problem we have been working on—one that needs immediate consideration and action. The problem is a serious one; it is called the 1970 Census. Over the course of the past year, I have had repeated correspondence with Mr. Ross Eckler, Director of the Bureau of the Census, in an effort to have included in the 1970 Census a question concerning which language is currently spoken in the home if it is not English.

The response from Mr. Eckler has been overwhelming; I have been overwhelmed with understanding and sympathy, but not with action.

Mr. Eckler assures me that he does intend to run a special *sample survey* directed to this issue, but then adds that because of the problems involved in administering the 1970 Census, the special *sample survey* will be delayed until after the 1970 Census has been taken. So, we are talking about years passing before we can get any kind of accurate assessment of the dimensions of the problem with which we are attempting to cope.

Recently, I have taken this matter up with an authority higher than Mr. Eckler; we shall see what the result is. In any event, this is a matter to which you might wish to address yourselves in a formal manner. You and your organizations carry considerable weight. We need all the weight we can stack together to move the Bureau of the Census on this bilingual question.

There are several broad areas in the field of bilingual education that I think Congress should address itself to during the months ahead. To help with our discussions in Congress, I want the benefit of your thinking on problem areas which I would like to enumerate; areas which suggest possible amendments to the Bilingual Education Act.

Presently, as on the books, the Bilingual Education Act fails to include bilingual education programs for American Indian children living on reservations and attending schools run by the Bureau of Indian Affairs. If the Indian child happens to live in Los Angeles and is attending the Los Angeles County school system, then it is possible for him to participate in a bilingual education program; but schools run by the Bureau of Indian Affairs are now excluded from participation in the Act.

This seems a manifest injustice when we note that there are approximately 50,000 young Indian children in federal schools, with about 10,000 more Indian children entering the first and other primary grades each year. About 80 percent of these children come to these schools speaking only an Indian language, or speaking such a minimal amount of English that for all practical purposes they are monolingual. Therefore, I am considering proposing expanded coverage by the Act to include these Indian children.

Recently, as a ranking member of the Education Subcommittee of the Senate Committee on Labor and Public Welfare, I conducted three days of hearings in California and Texas on the problems faced by the Mexican-American elderly. These hearings were most productive and informative.

One thing we learned was most shocking; only a very few persons employed by the federal government are trained bilingually. I am speaking here of those persons whose jobs *demand* that they have this kind of linguistic facility. The federal establishment, it appears, is making little or no effort to improve this situation.

The Committee received considerable testimony detailing the very serious problems faced by senior citizens who cannot break through the language barrier. The problems are obvious, ranging from inability to read or comprehend a contract of sale, to the inability to keep informed of job opportunities of federal programs. This testimony suggests to me that perhaps the concept of the Bilingual Education Act should be expanded so that bilingual education is also incorporated into the Adult Basic Education Act—so that adults may receive the benefits of a bilingual education. Additionally, the Congress is going to have to take a hard look at the federal administration of various programs, not only in education, but in many other fields, to see to it that in places where bilingual staff are required to do a job, such staff are hired, trained, and used.

Finally, the Congress needs the benefit of your thinking in another area of language education; one, which under a strict definition of terms might not qualify as bilingual education, but which nonetheless poses many problems for the children involved. Specifically, I am referring to the problem of dialect among the Negro children of our ghettos. The fact of the matter is that the vast majority of Negro youngsters speak the language of their community—a variety of English which has adopted certain features of pronunciation and grammar that differ from those of other dialects (just as these differ from still others) but which are understood and are effective within the community of speakers. But once that youngster steps outside of his community and attempts to get a job that is more than menial, he is faced not only with the problems that a child of Mexican-American or French-Canadian descent faces, and inability to reach others, but with the very special suspicions that speakers of one dialect always reserve for speakers of another: that the difference is due to "ignorance." We are often more ready to accept a distinctly foreign accent than a native accent that in our pride of speech we do not deign to regard as standard.

In a sense, the Negro child must learn to operate in two worlds—
that of his community and that of the economic and social complex
beyond his community. The fact that many Negroes seem to others
to be speaking poor English only reflects the *social* standing of their
dialect, not its linguistic standing or its natural utility. Nevertheless,
it is to their benefit to learn another dialect, and they would long
since have been able to do this had the educational system been
geared to the need. There is no doubt that the language barrier faced
by the youngsters of the ghetto is in every sense as real and as
impenetrable as that faced by the child who speaks no English at all;
he is penalized by the educational system, chastised as being ignorant, and turned down when he seeks any kind of employment that
involves communication.

What needs to be examined, however, is how we might best deal
with this problem. I turn to you, as the experts, for your assistance.
Help me, my staff, the committees I serve on, and the Congress to
find out what is going on—what the various theoretical and practical
considerations for a plan of action are—and work with us once again
in passing legislation designed to improve our society.

You people were among the leading lights that helped to make the
Bilingual Education Act possible; and I thank you for your counsel
and your efforts on behalf of that bill. The time has come to
strengthen that which we have put together. We need more money;
we need more information through the Census; we need expanded
coverage of Indian children and non-English-speaking adults; we need
a greater effort by the federal bureaucracy to seek bilingual staff; and
we need some kind of action to help the child of the ghetto.

I have been suggesting amendments to the Bilingual Education
Act—amendments designed to perfect the law as it now stands, and
designed to improve the lot of those persons whom the law is capable
of serving. It strikes me that all of us are in the business of improving
one thing or another. My improving is done through legislation;
yours is done through scholarship and teaching. And I think that
through your efforts to understand and improve our knowledge of
and ability to use languages you are performing the most fundamental and important task of civilizing man.

Language is at best a crude and imprecise tool to reflect and
express the infinitely subtle ramifications of our thoughts. But in our

increased understanding of the semantic imprecision of language lies our conviction to understand: nations must learn to understand nations; peoples must learn to understand peoples; and man must learn to understand his fellowman. It is through language—perhaps through language alone—that this understanding can be achieved.

In many ways we are prisoners of our tongues; faced with beauty or faced with terror, words escape us. Perhaps that is a blessing, for as we attempt to give words to our thoughts we all too often fail, and because of our failure to communicate effectively there is hatred and mistrust. Sometimes there is war.

And so, I view your mission as scholars and teachers of languages as one of prime importance. When the light of learning is kindled in a child, when that child embraces and masters his own language and then goes on and gains understanding of other tongues, a foundation for understanding is being laid. With each discovery of nuance or shade of meaning, his ability *to communicate* is strengthened. This is why, as you proceed with your endeavors, you should know that you have both my gratitude and my respect.

8. Bilingual Education in a Sociolinguistic Perspective

Joshua A. Fishman and John Lovas

As bilingual education programs developed in the United States in 1968 and 1969, it became necessary to clarify the term and the concepts behind it. Two useful surveys have appeared: *Early Childhood Bilingual Education*, by Vera P. John and Vivian M. Horner (New York: MLA, 1971) and *Bilingual Schooling in the United States*, by Theodore Andersson and Mildred Boyer (Washington: GPO, 2 vols., 1970). The latter reprinted a thorough typology of bilingual education by Professor William Mackey, who set out all the possible models of programs. In the paper that follows, Professors Fishman and Lovas emphasize that educational goals must be based on an understanding of the society for which they are developed: they outline four broad categories of bilingual education and discuss the implications of each. Joshua A. Fishman is Research Professor of Social Sciences at Yeshiva University and Visiting Professor at the Hebrew University; John Lovas teaches in the Language Arts Department of Foothill College, Los Altos, California. This paper was read at the 1970 TESOL Convention.

Bilingual education in the United States currently suffers from three serious lacks: a lack of funds (Title VII is pitifully starved), a lack of personnel (there are almost no optimally trained personnel in this field), and lack of evaluated programs (curricula, material, methods). However, all in all, we are not discouraged. We live in an age of miracles. If we have reached the stage where even teachers of English as a Second Language are becoming genuinely interested in bilingual education then, truly, the remaining hurdles should soon fall away and the millenium arrive in our own days!

As public educational agencies finally begin to develop programs

Reprinted from *the TESOL Quarterly*, 4, 1970, pages 215-22, by permission of the authors and the publishers.

in bilingual education for the "other-than-English-speaking" communities in the United States, those who are committed to the notion that cultural diversity is a natural and valuable asset to this country (and the world) might be expected to simply set up a cheer of approval and to urge that we get on with this shamefully delayed task without further delay. Though I number myself among these who value the maintenance and development of cultural and linguistic diversity in the United States, it is not entirely clear to me that *that* is what most of the existing and proposed bilingual education programs have as their goal. Further, even those programs that do explicitly state goals of language and culture maintenance often seem to overlook an important dimension in planning their efforts, an oversight which could seriously limit the success of these bilingual programs per se.

Needed: Realistic Societal Information for Realistic Educational Goals

Since most existing bilingual education programs in the United States provide only educational, psychological, or linguistic rationales for their efforts, the insights into societal bilingualism recently advanced by sociolinguists have not yet been incorporated into their designs. Thus, many programs are attempting language shift or language maintenance with little or no conscious awareness of the complexity of such an effort when viewed from a societal perspective.

Let us try to be more explicit about the kinds of difficulties that may develop for bilingual education programs if school planners are not aware of the language situations in the communities to which these programs are directed:

1. The school may attempt a program aimed at language maintenance (e.g., developing high performance in all skill areas of mother tongue and second language, and promoting use of both languages in all major societal domains) in a community actually in the process of language shift. Thus, the school's efforts could be canceled out because it did not take account of community values or preferences.

2. Conversely, the school may attempt a program aimed at language shift (e.g., developing competence in the second language only and extending its use to all major domains) for a community determined to maintain its own language in many (or

all) social domains. Again, the school could fail (or achieve very limited success) because it ignored the sociolinguistic dimension of the problem.

3. Even if the school program and community objectives are fortuitously congruent, the school program may not take account of important characteristics of the speech community, e.g., (a) the existence of one or more nonstandard varieties (in one or more languages) whose school appropriateness as a medium or as a subject must be ascertained from the speech community itself; (b) differential use of these varieties by members of the speech community from one societal domain to another and from one speech network to another.

Schools often adopt simplistic notions, e.g., that there is only one "real" kind of Spanish and one "real" kind of English and that everyone everywhere uses (or should use) this "one kind." Such notions are obviously untrue.

Four Broad Categories of Bilingual Education Programs

It may be instructive to propose a tentative typology of bilingual education programs based on differing kinds of community and school objectives. Each of these types will be briefly illustrated by an existing or proposed bilingual education program for some Spanish-speaking community. In presenting this typology of bilingual education programs, I would like to distinguish clearly between them and English-as-a-second-language programs. The latter are programs which include no instruction in the student's mother tongue as part of the program. Andersson (1968) makes this point quite clear:

> Bilingual education in a Spanish-speaking area may be defined quite simply as that form of schooling which uses both Spanish and English as media of instruction. Bilingual schooling has often been confused with the teaching of English as a second language (ESL).

Another point about this typology is that it is *not* based on student and schedule characteristics such as proportion of students speaking a certain language and proportion of time devoted to each language (Gaarder, 1967; Michel, 1967; Andersson, 1968). Rather it looks to the kinds of sociolinguistic development implied in the program objectives, and suggests that various kinds of programs assume and lead to particular societal roles for the languages taught.

Type I. *Transitional Bilingualism.* In such a program Spanish is used in the early grades to the extent necessary to allow pupils to "adjust to school" and/or to "master subject matter" until their skill in English is developed to the point that it alone can be used as the medium of instruction. Such programs do not strive toward goals of fluency and literacy in both languages with opportunity throughout the curriculum for the continued improved mastery of each. Rather, they state goals such as "increasing overall achievement of Spanish-speaking students by using both Spanish and English as media of instruction in the primary grades." Such programs (consciously or unconsciously) correspond to a societal objective of language shift and give no consideration to long-range institutional development and support of the mother tongue. An example of such a program can be found in the grant proposal of the Los Cruces (N.M.) School District No. 2 for support of their Sustained Primary Program for Bilingual Students. Perhaps the best way to characterize this program would be to cite the three primary objectives against which the program is to be evaluated:

1. To increase the achievement level of Spanish-speaking young-sters through the use of a sustained K-3 program.
2. To determine whether Spanish-speaking youngsters achieve more in a program that utilizes instruction in both Spanish and English or in a program that is taught in Spanish only.
3. To involve the parents of the Spanish-speaking students in the educational program as advisors and learners, thus enriching the home environment of the child.

The entire proposal makes no mention of measuring performance in Spanish, or continuing Spanish in the curriculum past grade 3, or of making any survey of the language situation in the community.[1] Such programs are basically interested only in transitional bilingual-ism, i.e., in arriving at the stage of English monolingual educational normality just as soon as is feasible without injuring the pupil or arousing the community.

---

[1] Other transitional programs, as mentioned by John and Horner (1971), are the Follow-Through Project at Corpus Christi, Texas, and the various informal programs for Puerto Rican students in New York City and elsewhere which depend on the use of "community aides" in the classroom.

Type II. *Monoliterate Bilingualism.* Programs of this type indicate goals of development in both languages for aural-oral skills, but do not concern themselves with literacy skills in the mother tongue. Thus, such programs emphasize developing fluency in Spanish as a link between home and school, with the school providing recognition and support for the language in the domains of home and neighborhood; but it does not concern itself with the development of literacy skills in the non-English mother tongue which would increase the formal domains in which the child could use the language. This type of program is intermediate in orientation between language shift and language maintenance. The likely societal effect of such a program might be one of language maintenance in the short run, but, given the exposure of students to American urban society which stresses and rewards literacy, it might well lead to shift. One example of such a program can be found in Christine McDonald's proposal for the El Rancho Unified School District in Pico Rivera, California. The program is designed for preschool children and their parents, and would focus particularly on reading-readiness activities. The proposal envisions a teacher fluent in Spanish and acceptance of the parents' and children's home language. However, the focus of the program would be on ultimately developing literacy in English with no reference to similar development in Spanish. Bilingual programs for American Indians frequently fall into this category, because, in many instances, there is no body of written literature for the child to learn in his mother tongue. Obviously the intellectual imbalance between English literacy and mother tongue illiteracy poses a difficult situation for any maintenance-oriented community, particularly if it is exposed to occupational mobility through English.

Type III. *Partial Bilingualism.* This kind of program seeks fluency and literacy in both languages, but literacy in the mother tongue is restricted to certain subject matter, most generally that related to the ethnic group and its cultural heritage. In such a program, reading and writing skills in the mother tongue are commonly developed in relation to the social sciences, literature, and the arts, but not in science and mathematics.[2] This kind of program is clearly one of language maintenance coupled with a certain effort at culture maintenance

---

[2] The Rough Rock Demonstration School (Navajo) initially tended to follow a program of this kind (John and Horner, 1971).

(perhaps even cultural development should the program result in the production of poetry and other literary art forms). In general, the program in the Dade County (Florida) Public Schools (as described in its administrative guide lines and also in Rojas, 1966) exemplifies this type of bilingual education. The program provides special instruction in English in all skills for all Spanish-speaking students who need it. Additionally, the program provides formal instruction in reading and writing Spanish with emphasis on Spanish literature and civilization as subject matter. Other areas of the curriculum do not utilize Spanish as a medium of instruction. Other programs of this type are conducted by numerous American ethnic groups in their own supplementary or parochial schools (Fishman, 1966). Such programs imply that while the non-English mother tongues are serious vehicles of modern literate thought, they are not related to control of the technological and economic spheres. The latter are considered to be the preserve of the majority, whose language must be mastered if these spheres are to be entered. Nationalist protest movements since the mid-nineteenth century have consistently rejected any such limiting implication.[3]

Type IV. *Full Bilingualism.* In this kind of program, students are to develop all skills in both languages in all domains. Typically, both languages are used as media of instruction for all subjects (except in teaching the languages themselves). Clearly this program is directed at language maintenance and development of the minority language. From the viewpoint of much of the linguistically and psychologically oriented literature, this is the ideal type of program, as illustrated by these comments:

> Since one of our purposes is as nearly as possible to form and educate balanced, coordinate bilinguals—children capable of thinking and feeling in either of two languages independently— instruction should, we believe, be given in both languages . . . (Michel, 1967)
>
> An education, both in and out of school, which respects these basic principles [to gain "progressive control of both languages" and "a sympathetic understanding of both cultures"] should

---

[3]Mackey (1969) refers to such limited bilingual programs as being of the "Dual-Medium Differential Maintenance" Type.

hopefully produce after us a generation of bilinguals who really are fully bilingual as well as bicultural. (Andersson, 1967)

Programs such as these enable us to examine the difference between developing *balanced competency in individuals* and producing a *balanced bilingual society.* Though bilingual societies might find individuals with highly developed competency in all skills and domains very useful in a variety of interlocutor roles (teachers, translators, business representatives), a fully balanced bilingual speech community seems to be a theoretical impossibility because balanced competence implies languages that are functionally equivalent and no society can be motivated to maintain two languages if they are really functionally redundant. Thus, this type of program does not seem to have a clearly articulated goal with respect to *societal* reality.

Several examples of this type of program exist, but all of them are small pilot or experimental programs. The Coral Way Elementary School (Dade County, Florida) and the Laredo Unified Consolidated Independent School District (Texas) are two frequently cited instances which exemplify this kind of program (Gaarder, 1967; Michel, 1967; Andersson, 1968). In the Coral Way School, students receive instruction in all subjects in both languages, English in the morning from one teacher, Spanish in the afternoon from another teacher. At Laredo Unified, students receive all instruction from the same teacher who uses English half the day and Spanish the other half. The evidence so far suggests that these programs are quite successful, but looking at them from the view of the functional needs of the community, there is serious question whether they should serve as ideal models for large-scale programs. As social policy they may well be self-defeating in that they require and often lead to significant social separation for their maintenance rather than merely for their origin.[4]

Needed: Societal Information in Establishing a Bilingual Education Program

---

[4]Mackey (1969) has dubbed such programs as being "dual-medium equal maintenance" in type. The Rough Rock Demonstration School currently tends in this direction.

Various types of bilingual education programs make implicit assumptions about the kind of language situation that exists in a given community and about the kind of language situation that ought to exist in that community. Program developers should make their assumptions explicit and attempt to test the validity of these assumptions by gathering various kinds of data regarding the societal functions of community languages and existing attitudes toward them, both before and during the development of bilingual education programs.

Gaarder (1967) suggests that the way in which a school or community goes about establishing a bilingual program will largely define the structure the program will take. That assumption underlies the suggestions here for gathering information beyond that normally available in school records and county census data as part of the process of deciding whether to establish a bilingual program and what kind of program to establish, if the first decision is affirmative. In this early stage of development the following information seems minimal, if the school and community are going to make conscious, explicit decisions about an appropriate bilingual program:

1. A survey that would establish the languages and varieties employed by both parents and children, by societal domain or function.
2. Some rough estimate of their relative performance level in each language, by societal domain.
3. Some indication of community (and school staff) attitudes toward the existing languages and varieties, and toward their present allocation to domains.
4. Some indication of community (and school staff) attitudes toward changing the existing language situation.[5]

This information would allow citizens, board members, administrators, and teachers to decide which type of program (or combination of program types) would be most appropriate to the community, both in terms of the *existing* language situation and in terms of the *direction and extent of change* in that situation.

---

[5] For an introduction to domain-related applied sociolinguistic description see Fishman, Cooper, and Ma (1968). For the theory underlying such description see Fishman (1967).

Once a decision to develop a program is made, more detailed information would be required, particularly for determining the materials and methods most appropriate to achieving the program's objectives. Such information might include the following:

1. A contrastive analysis of the major languages and/or varieties used in the community and any languages or varieties being introduced in the school.
2. An analysis of the phonological, grammatical, and lexical variables that most clearly distinguish varieties.
3. More detailed measures of student performance by language and domain.

Data of this sort would allow curriculum specialists and in-service training instructors to choose and/or develop instructional materials and methods appropriate to the students in the community, ideally avoiding the traps of (a) teaching them what they *already* know or (b) teaching them what they don't want at the expense of *developing greater skill in the domains which the community recognizes and wants developed.*

Conclusions

After a hiatus of more than half a century (Fishman, 1968) we are just now reentering the first stages of genuine bilingual education at public expense. We are just overcoming the deceptive and self-deluding view that teaching English as a second language is, in itself, all there is to bilingual education. We are just beginning to seriously ponder different curricular models of real bilingual education. This paper stresses that such models have societal implications, make societal assumptions, and require societal data for their implementation and evaluation.

We are just beginning to realize that public schools should belong to parents, to pupils, to communities. We are just beginning to suspect that these may be legitimately interested in more than learning English and affording better and bigger TV sets. We may soon arrive at the disturbing conclusion that it is not necessarily treasonous for pupils, teachers, parents, and principals to speak to each other in languages other than English, even when they *are* in school, even when they *know* English too, and even when the languages involved are their *own mother tongues!*

However, we still have a very long way to go. We still do not realize that the need for bilingual education must not be viewed as merely a disease of the poor and the disadvantaged. We still do not realize that alternative curricular approaches to bilingual education make tacit assumptions and reach tacit decisions concerning the social roles of the languages (or language varieties) to be taught. We still do not realize that these assumptions and decisions can be empirically confirmed or disconfirmed by sociolinguistic data pertaining to the communities that our programs claim to serve. By and large, we still do not know how to collect the societal data we need for enlightened decision making in the field of bilingual education.

We are learning all of these things the hard way—which may be the only way important lessons are learned in the world of public education—but we are learning! Thank God for poor Mexican-American parents and their increasingly short tempers. Because of their number and their growing organization our grandchildren have a chance of getting a bilingual public education in the United States without necessarily being either poor or even Hispanic.

REFERENCES

Andersson, Theodore. "The Bilingual in the Southwest." *Florida FL Reporter,* 5:2 (1967), 3.
———. "Bilingual Elementary Schooling: A Report to Texas Educators." *Florida FL Reporter,* 6:2 (1968), 3-4 ff.
———, and Mildred Boyer. *Bilingual Schooling in the United States.* Washington, D.C. USGPO, 1970.
Fishman, J. A. *Language Loyalty in the United States,* Chapter 5: "The Ethnic Group School and Mother Tongue Maintenance," pp. 92-126. The Hague: Mouton, 1966.
———. "Bilingualism With and Without Diglossia; Diglossia With and Without Bilingualism." *Journal of Social Issues,* 23 (1967), 29-38.
———. "The Breadth and Depth of English in the United States." *Language and Language Learning.* Ed. Albert H. Marckwardt. National Council of Teachers of English, 1968, pp. 43-53.
———. R. L. Cooper, Roxana Ma et al, *Bilingualism in the Barrio,* New York, Yeshiva University, Report to USOE under contract OEC-1-7-062817-0297, 1968; also Bloomington, Ind., *Language Sciences Series,* 1971.
Gaarder, A. B. "Organization of the Bilingual School." *Journal of Social Issues,* 23 (1967), 110-120.
John, Vera, and Vivian Horner. *Early Childhood Bilingual Education.* New York: MLA, 1971.

Las Cruces School District No. 2, Las Cruces, New Mexico: *Sustained Primary Program for Bilingual Students,* ERIC No. ED 001 869.

Mackey, William F. "A Typology of Bilingual Education," *Foreign Language Annals,* 3 (1970): 596-608.

McDonald, Christina. *A Tentative Program for Combining the Education of Preschool Mexican-American Children with Parent Education.* Pico Rivera, Calif.: El Rancho Unified School District, 1964.

Michel, Joseph. "Tentative Guidelines for a Bilingual Curriculum." *Florida FL Reporter,* 5:3 (1967), 13-16.

Planning for Non-English Speaking Pupils. Miami: Dade County Public Schools, 1963. ERIC No. 002 529.

Preschool Instructional Program for Non-English Speaking Children. Austin: Texas Educational Agency, 1964. ERIC No. ED 001 091.

Pryor, G. C. *Evaluation of the Bilingual Project of Harlandale Independent School District, San Antonio, Texas in the First and Second Grades of Four Elementary Schools During 1967-68 School Year.* San Antonio: Our Lady of the Lake College, 1968.

Rojas, Pauline. "The Miami Experience in Bilingual Education." *On Teaching English to Speakers of Other Languages, Series II.* Ed. Virginia F. Allen. National Council of Teachers of English, 1966, pp. 43-45.

9. Bilingual Education Programs in the United States: For Assimilation or Pluralism?

Rolf Kjolseth

Most of those who speak in favor of bilingual education programs include an argument for replacing the American ideal of the melting pot by the acceptance of cultural pluralism. The following paper by Professor Kjolseth points out that in practice the vast majority of programs in existence aim at assimilation to the dominant culture rather than preservation of ethnic differences. They intend to permit members of the minority language groups to enter the majority culture, but set as a condition that they give up their own language. Rolf Kjolseth is associate professor of sociology at the University of Colorado, Boulder.

Recent legislation[1] and financial support[2] for bilingual education programs in the United States are held by many to indicate a basic liberal breakaway from an earlier "language policy" and social context which successfully assimilated several waves of the most diverse immigrant groups into mainstream monolingual American society.

This article, printed with the permission of the author, is a revised version of a paper originally presented in the section on "Sociological Perspectives on Bilingual Education" of the Sociolinguistics Program at the Seventh World Congress of Sociology held in Varna, Bulgaria, September 14-19, 1970, and will appear in the *Acts* of the Congress. The revised version will also be published in R. Kjolseth and F. Sack (eds.), *Zur Soziologie der Sprache: Ausgewaehlte Schriften vom VII. Weltkingress der Soziologie,* to appear as a special issue of *Koelner Zeitschrift fuer Soziologie und Sozialpsychologie,* November-December 1971.

[1] Federal legislation was enacted January 2, 1968, as Title VII of the Elementary and Secondary Education Act of 1965. The text of this law is reproduced by Andersson (1970, vol. 2, 1-6).

[2] Although forty-five million dollars was authorized for the first three fiscal years, actual appropriations, which are granted on a one-year basis, have been only half of that authorized. Fishman (1970) discusses the politics involved.

One often hears, especially from those who in one capacity or another are promoting these new programs, that they will favor cultural bilingualism and pluralism, that is, the democratic coexistence of ethnic and nonethnic groups.

This paper seeks to critically examine this thesis within a sociolinguistic perspective which, necessarily, considers the relevance and effects of bilingual programs upon language use beyond the school within the wider community.

However, an analysis of specific programs must first be prefaced by a few introductory remarks. These will touch upon the role of the school in community social change, sketch the concepts and method by which the analysis will proceed, and very briefly describe the social context of the communities in which these bilingual programs are embedded.

It would be a mistake to overestimate what any school can accomplish or to overvalue the significance of a student's performance if it is restricted only to the domain of the school itself. The school is only one domain in the life space of individuals and communities. Language cannot "live" there, although it may receive important impulses. The life of a language depends first and foremost upon its use[3] in other domains. When a person has skills in two languages, this individual bilingualism, if it is to be stable, must be sustained by diglossic[4] norms of community language use (Fishman, 1967). Hence

---

[3] Sociolinguistic research has clearly shown that there is no necessary, invariable, or universal correlation between *attitudes* toward a language (ethnolinguistics) and actual patterns of language *use* (dominance configuration) within a speech community. For an early treatment of language use patterns see Schmidt-Rohr (1933, 178-92). Landmann (1968) offers a fascinating historical account of a case (Yiddish) where negative attitudes concurred with increasing use of the ethnic language and vice versa. Nevertheless, there is presently an inordinate research emphasis upon attitudes which tacitly assumes them to be adequate indicators of language behavior.

[4] "Diglossia," coined by Ferguson (1959) and expanded by Gumperz (1964) and Fishman (1965, 1967, 1971) describes or characterizes a society wherein two or more language varieties are normatively employed, each for separate, complementary functions or domains. Diglossia is therefore a multilingual "opportunity structure" which sustains bilingualism in individuals who, as they move from a social context dominated by one language to another dominated by norms of appropriateness for a second language, will be constrained to switch idioms and so in the normal round of everyday life will use both languages and thereby naturally maintain their bilingualism through the only means possible—use.

a bilingual program which fosters bilingual use outside the school and norms of stable and balanced diglossia is one which can be said to promote linguistic pluralism, whereas a program which restricts or inhibits bilingual use in other than school domains and erodes diglossic community norms is one which must be characterized as promoting linguistic assimilation.

In other words, a bilingual program's social effectiveness is seen in the school domain's qualitative and quantitative effect upon the *use* of each language in other community domains.

Hard evidence on varying programs' differential effects upon community language-use patterns must come from comparative empirical community research of diachronic shifts in the dominance configurations of specific groups. However, prior to this, a provisional and substitute route via secondary research can be used to cast some light on the question of the likely effects of bilingual programs as currently structured.

We can consider any bilingual program as being composed of a set of structural options resulting from basic policy decisions. I have considered a large set and selected a nonexclusive subset of some fifteen which appear most relevant[5] in terms of having a potential effect upon language use outside the school. Thus each of these options is held to be potentially relevant in affecting language use within the community either in the direction of ethnic language maintenance or shift depending upon whether or not the option is taken and/or how it is filled or operationalized.

To simplify this presentation, all the options judged likely to produce ethnic language shift can be collected into an ideal-typical and extreme "assimilation model" and all those options which tend to foster ethnic language maintenance into a polar "pluralistic model." These two models therefore represent two extremes on a continuum of possible structures of bilingual education programs.

However, before presenting the two models, a number of contextual restrictions are in order because it must be clear that no feature of a bilingual education program can be considered shift- or maintenance-fostering in and of itself. It is only within specific sociocultural contexts of great complexity that any program feature takes on relevance in one direction or the other.

[5] Gaarder (1967) discusses some of these program options, as does Mackey (1970).

Although these contextual features themselves merit an entire essay, I can only index a few here in order to suggest the frame of reference to which this analysis is restricted.

To speak of bilingual programs in the United States, the site of one of the most massive language shifts in world history while half the world's population is characterized by stable intragroup bilingualism (Macnamara, 1967), is to speak of quite a special case. Furthermore, I will restrict the context of my remarks to bilingual programs for Spanish-speaking Americans—the nation's largest foreign language minority and second largest ethnic minority[6]—with particular reference to Mexican Americans, or, as many more recently prefer to designate themselves, Chicanos.

This group's ancestors came as colonial conquerors in the sixteenth century and were in turn conquered in the nineteenth century.[7] Since then Mexican Americans have continued to grow in numbers through natural increase[8] and continuing immigration.[9]

---

[6]Estimates vary because the government has not included language items in its census questionnaires and has grouped Mexican Americans together with "whites." The Mexican American Population Commission of California places the number of "Americans of Hispanic origin" at 9.2 million as of 1971. "Hispanic origin" includes, in order of relative magnitude Mexicans, Puerto Ricans, Cubans, and other Latin Americans. By conservative estimate (John and Horner, 1971, 2) there were over 4 million Mexican Americans in the United States by 1971. Fishman (1966, 42) estimates 3.4 million claimants of Spanish as their mother tongue in 1960.

[7]Don Juan de Onate arrived on the banks of the Rio Grand river on Ascension Day, 1598, claiming all the eye beheld for Spain (Steiner, 1969, 331-32). Mexican hegemony was broken by the war between Mexico and the United States in 1846, which United States General Ulysses S. Grant characterized as the "most unjust [war] ever waged by a stronger against a weaker nation." (Steiner, 1969, 362). As a consequence Mexico lost what has since become Texas, New Mexico, Arizona, and much of California, Nevada, Utah, and Colorado—an area comprising one-third of the United States (Steiner, 1969, 57).

[8]According to the 1960 U.S. census, the median age of Mexican Americans was 17 years and their high birth rate is reflected in 709 children under 5 years of age per 1,000 women age 15 to 49 (compared to 613 for Blacks and 455 for Anglos).

[9]The periods of largest immigration were 1920-29 (487,775) and 1955-64 (432,573). A number of factors such as the elimination of the "bracero" program (post 1965) and the extremely rapid mechanization and automation of all industries, including agricultural, has severely reduced job opportunities for the unskilled and has considerably reduced more recent immigration.

They are concentrated primarily in urban centers in five South-western states[10] and possess a rich folk culture.[11] The overwhelming majority are poor[12] ("lower-class"), politically powerless,[13] sharply discriminated against, and residentially segregated whether in urban or rural settings. Furthermore, Spanish is only a prestige idiom in the United States where there are irrelevant numbers of Spanish speakers. Where Spanish speakers are a relatively large group, it is an idiom held in considerable contempt.[14]

These few indicators only suggest some of the principal dimensions of the social context which must be kept in mind as we now

[10]The 1960 census estimates that 87.2% of the Mexican origin population lives in the Southwest: California 40.1%, Arizona 6.0%, Colorado 1.2%, New Mexico 2.0%, and Texas 37.9% (Loyo, 1969, 35). They are primarily urban dwellers: 85.4% in California and New Mexico, 69.3% in Arizona, and 78.6% in Texas (Steiner, 1969, 42).

[11]This oral culture is now beginning to be collected and published in the Chicanco press, especially such periodicals as *Con Safos, La Raza,* and *El Grito.* Steiner (1969), 405-06) lists the addresses of twenty-six newspapers. Romano (1969) has recently edited a collection of native Chicano literature.

[12]Only 4.6% of the Mexican Americans were professionals (vs 15.1% for Anglos) according to the 1960 census. Taking all white-collar jobs together (professional, managerial, proprietors, sales, and clerical) 19% of the Mexican-American population held such positions vs. 46.8% of the Anglos. Of all Spanish-surnamed families in the Southwest in 1960, 34.8% were estimated as living at or below the "poverty level" meaning their annual family income was less than $3,000 in 1959 (Loyo, 1969, 78).

[13]For example, although one million Mexicans and Mexican Americans live in Los Angeles, making it the third largest "Mexican" city in the world (after Mexico City and Guadalajara), districts have been so completely gerrymandered that they do not have a single representative on the City Council (Steiner, 1969, 188-89).

[14]This might by formulated as "the Law of Anglo love of ethnic irrelevance," or the "Disneyland preference for symbolic ethnicity," i.e., the more locally irrelevant an ethnic language and culture is, the higher its social status, and the more viable it is locally, the lower its social status. Fishman (1966) has noted this attitude in the United States with respect to the most diverse ethnic languages and concluded that "as long as these languages and cultures are truly 'foreign' our schools are comfortable with them. But as soon as they are found in our own back yards, the schools deny them." This amounts to honoring the dead while burying the living.

consider first the pluralistic and then the assimilation models of bilingual education programs.

The Pluralistic Model

This program is one initiated by a group of ethnic and nonethnic community leaders in consultation with teachers and school administrators who form a continuing committee to both advise and control the program's operation. The bilingual program is a social issue around which the ethnic community becomes politically mobilized. The program's administration provides reciprocal control between the school and the community. Its reception and development are thereby tied into community decision making and public opinion formation.

Before the program is actually begun, empirical research is conducted locally to ascertain: 1) the dominance configuration of the ethnic and nonethnic languages for several social categories of speakers in the community, 2) the linguistic features of the specific varieties of ethnic language spoken locally, and 3) the attitudes of various social categories of community residents toward both the local and nonlocal ethnic language varieties. These investigations thus provide locally valid information which is utilized in the planning of the program components such as: the selection of linguistic varieties to be included in the classroom repertoire, the choice of instructional materials, and the determination of teacher in-service training components. These investigations additionally provide baseline data for later diachronic evaluations of the program's effects upon community language and language-related variables of both a behavioral and attitudinal nature.

The teacher(s) and aides in the bilingual program are of local, ethnic origin, newly appointed to the program, and receive special training to develop their communicative competence in using local and regional ethnic varieties of language and culture, their knowledge of ethnolinguistics (partly based on the preprogram community research), mother-tongue instruction methods, and techniques for teaching English to speakers of other languages (TESOL).[15] The teachers live and are active in the local ethnic community and are members of the program's coordinating committee. Their cultural and linguistic ideologies favor, and their behavior manifests, stable biculturalism and bilingualism. In summary, the teachers are effective bilingual and bicultural role models for their students.

The bilingual program is "two-way" with members of both the ethnic and nonethnic groups learning in their and the other's language (Stern, 1963) and classes are ethnically mixed (nonethnic on a voluntary basis) from the beginning, or, if initially segregated, they become mixed by the third or fourth grade (Gaarder, 1967).

Initially the medium of instruction is dual, using the local ethnic and core group's dialects[16] and both are presented by the same

---

[15]Gaarder (1970) implies the desirability of separate teachers for each language. However, such a division would exemplify for the pupils a complete contradiction of the program's verbally stated goal of fostering true biculturals and bilinguals. In such a program pupils are enjoined to become what the actions of their teachers and aides manifest as impossible. Actions speak louder than words. Rosenthal and Jacobson (1968) have carefully demonstrated the impact of such nonverbal messages on pupils and their motivations. Naturally teacher and aide training is a serious problem. Equally important is the question, "What kind of training in which linguistic varieties of each language and with what level of literacy for specific grade level positions?"

[16]This option for beginning instruction in the medium of locally normative language varieties is predicated on the dictum that "language teaching should be based on the resources that the child brings to the classroom" (Labov, 1971, 55). The American Association of Teachers of Spanish and Portuguese has recently recommended that "Especially in the case of learners whose dialect differs markedly from world standard (Spanish), the first weeks, months—in some cases, the entire first year—should focus patiently on developing their self-confidence as speakers and writers and readers of their *own kind* of Spanish" (Gaarder, 1971, 5, emphasis in original). Note however that the everyday term "dialect"—as opposed to the sociolinguistic term "language variety"—always contains sociocultural and political judgments (Fishman, 1972). Hence social conflicts often become manifest in decisions about whether or not a particular language variety is to be considered a "dialect" or not. It is a curiosity that Gaarder (1971) includes Barker (1971) in his references as she opens her book with a scathing condemnation of Pachuco Spanish—a widespread ethnic language variety spoken in the Southwest. Careful empirical research on intralanguage varieties and their educational significance has been conducted bv Labov (1966), Stewart (1966, 1969), Dillard (1969), and Baratz and Shuy (1969) among others. Much of this work has focused on the varieties of English spoken by Blacks. Gumperz (1970a and 1970b, 1969a) has pioneered work on Chicano speech involving rapid Spanish/English switching and Kjolseth et al. (in preparation) are presently analyzing the grammar and social functions of such speech.

teacher. Each dialect receives equal time and equal treatment, initially through the presentation of a lesson in the student's strongest, or principal language variety, followed by presentation of the same materials in the second language variety, i.e., in the principal language variety of the nonethnic children.[17] Later when students have a better command of the second language variety, the class may alternate from one to the other without doubling or repeating the same materials in the other. Physical education and play periods permit the use of all language varieties. Some programs may later develop towards using the two linguistic varieties for separate but essential and socially significant subject areas without relegating either to unimportant purposes. Gradually the two standard varieties (ethnic and nonethnic) are introduced but never completely supplant some use of the dialects[18] and do not disturb the overall ethnic to nonethnic language balance. The development trend of the program, which lasts a minimum of nine years, is toward maintenance of both languages, i.e., all four varieties.[19]

The content of the bilingual curriculum stimulates ethnic community language-planning efforts and includes considerable attention to the local and regional cultures of both the ethnic and core groups in such a way as to provide a natural context for alternate use of both dialect and standard varieties. The results of research on local attitudes toward language varieties, their speakers, and bilingualism,[20] as well as information on vocational opportunities in edu-

---

Rayfield (1970) has analyzed similar switching patterns involving Yiddish and English.

[17]This is intended to facilitate the ethnic child's acquisition of a variety of the nonethnic language which is *appropriate* (Hymes, 1966, 22-23) in local peer level communication. Thus both ethnic and nonethnic puplis initially add a language variety to their linguistic repertoires which is appropriate for local communication with their outgroup peers, thereby favoring second language *use* by members of both groups in intergroup conversation outside the classroom.

[18]One place where "dialects" have an unquestionably appropriate place in classroom activities at all grade levels is that of creative writing, especially about relevant sociocultural topics.

[19]Of course, as the pupil progresses, new stylistic levels in both languages (informal, careful, formal, ceremonial) are added to the classroom repertoire.

[20]A clear understanding of the content and social basis for local prejudices against different language varieties and their speakers is essential for "nondefensive cultural self-defense."

cation, industry, commerce, and government requiring or facilitated by bilingualism are presented first indirectly, and later directly.[21]

Demonstration classes are held for parents from all groups to promote understanding of the bilingual program and its methods as well as to encourage interest in a parallel program of bilingual adult education. In general the adult program is organized in ways analogous to that of the students but with materials adjusted to the age group: ethnically mixed classes, dual medium with equal time and treatment of the language varieties, an early emphasis on dialects, preferably the same teacher and similar content areas as in the children's program, information on bilingual vocational counseling, and local attitudes toward language varieties and their speakers.

A number of extracurricular activities involve both parents and children from both groups; for example a lending library might be established with a variety of materials such as comics, magazines, newspapers, and books for a spectrum of interests, social-class levels, and age groups.

A series of public lectures and articles in local newspapers give information on the range of school and school-related programs, their rationale, organization, evaluation, and progress. Emphasis is placed on the program's interest in cultivating local varieties of language and culture for all groups. The community board of the bilingual program acts as the central controlling and coordinating body for this set of bilingual-bicultural activities in, near, and outside the school.

Evaluative research on the program considers not only changes in individual language skills and attitudes (as well as the traditional measures of academic achievement) but also tests for (sub-) *group qualitative and quantitative measures of the frequency of use of different language varieties in domains outside the school.* The emphasis is sociolinguistic.

The most important dimensions of the pluralistic bilingual program can be briefly summarized:

1) This program acts as a continuing stimulus to civic development and organization within the ethnic community and encourages

---

[21]Much more attention needs to be paid to presently nonexistent occupational categories which are, however, necessary in meeting the needs of the local ethnic community's majority.

a democratic forum for the resolution of conflicts and differing interests within and between the ethnic and nonethnic communities.

2) The teaching personnel are, on ascriptive, achieved, and behavioral grounds, credible exemplifications for ethnic and nonethnic students and parents of successfully operative bilinguals and biculturals.

3) Paralleling the composition of administrative control with its egalitarian distribution of power among diverse community interest groups, the linguistic and cultural content of the pluralistic program might be metaphorically characterized as "horizontally" articulated, emphasizing the complementarity of different varieties of situationally appropriate culture and language. This along with an increased awareness of ethnolinguistics encourages the student to become active in a variety of settings, use a number of linguistic varieties, and become experienced in switching between them. Language skills and cultural perspectives are added without progressively destroying his home language and culture. Furthermore, these developments take place in *both* groups. The success or failure of this program is most penetratingly indicated by the degree to which it encourages, engenders, and insures norms of appropriateness for non-English language varieties in community domains other than the school.[22]

The Assimilation Model

This bilingual program is initiated by the school without any community-based advanced planning. If a school-community advisory group is formed, it is without real powers to control the program. Community "involvement"[23] is encouraged and community control is avoided.

---

[22] Any program's goals are reflected in three principal places: 1) the program's *statement* of goals, 2) the program's *structure* or design options, and 3) the teleology, hypotheses, and *research emphasis* of the program's evaluative component. The first is the weakest of the three as an indicator of what the program is, in fact, striving for.

[23] "Community involvement" is presently a popular euphemism which veils nonreciprocal rights between professionals who "serve" and the laity who are "served." Lay members opine and recommend while professionals decide and execute. "Involvement" is a well-known management technique long used in industry and designed to give those most directly affected by policy the feeling of influence rather than real influence itself. The U.S. Office of Education's Title VII Manual (USOE, 1970, 31-34, and Andersson, 1970, vol. 2, 7-20) *requires* community "involvement" and fails to make any recommendation concerning

The teacher is either a nonethnic or, if a member of the ethnic group, one who lives in a nonethnic residential area and is either generally inactive in ethnic community affairs or active only in conservative elitist ethnic organizations and causes whose concerns and interests are distant from those which represent and speak to the basic everyday problems of the local ethnic majority. Transferred from some other class already within the school, this teacher will nevertheless have received some special in-service linguistic and cultural training for the position. This will not have included any significant concern for local ethnic culture, local language varieties (especially his or her competence in its *use*), or ethnolinguistics, but will have centered almost exclusively upon teaching a standard variety[24] of the ethnic language as a mother tongue (and as a medium of

---

community control. It is interesting to note that only two existing programs funded by the federal government have anything like clear community control features built into them: Coral Way and Rough Rock (John and Horner, 1971, 28-31 and 17-20 respectively). Each is also unique in another, perhaps very relevant way. Coral Way serves a community whose ethnic members are primarily "middle-class," i.e., close in social status to the educational professionals. Rough Rock on the other hand serves an exclusively Navajo community which is geographically very isolated from any nonethnic communities. For these reasons, neither provides a very relevant example because most programs are located in urban areas with a high concentration of "lower" class ethnics. Much more exemplary for having some community control features and a strong bilingual curriculum are Public Schools 25 and 155 in New York City (John and Horner, 1971, 52-56).

[24]This standard variety may be careful or formal "middle-class" Mexico City Spanish, "world Spanish" (Gaarder, 1971), or even academic Castilian Spanish. All are likely to be related to, but very distant from the locally appropriate and most frequently used ethnic language varieties of the Chicano community where a federally funded program is located, especially as the law requires demonstrating a concentration of ethnic families with annual family incomes below $3,000!

At a bilingual school in southern California in 1971 this writer was informed by a bilingual aide, who lived in the Mexican-American barrio, that she and the other first grade aids "envied" the "more correct" Spanish of the master teacher, who does not live in the barrio. One of the first grade readers being used (published in Madrid) was found to contain many vocabulary items (four on one particular page) which a "middle-class" Mexican college graduate would not understand. The master teacher admitted having had to look up these terms in her dictionary—also published in Madrid. The terms were nevertheless justified as "better Spanish" although they are obviously inappropriate in any natural speech setting locally.

It should be added that we are notoriously ignorant about what actually happens in classroom interaction and what language varieties are actually included in the classroom repertoire. Lewis (1970) offers a seminal exploratory study of problems of cross-cultural communication between teachers and students.

instruction) and the language's "high" culture. The teacher's attitudes with respect to language tend to be exclusive and purist, viewing "interference," whether from the ethnic dialect or English, as a major "problem" and local dialect as categorically improper and "incorrect."[25] Biculturalism of "high" culture and bilingualism of the "proper" variety are held to be worthy goals attainable only with great effort by his students, who are held to suffer from "cultural deprivation."[26]

---

[25] The "high/low" metaphor in popular usage characterizing linguistic and cultural varieties as well as social classes is, unfortunately, often uncritically adopted into the working vocabulary of social science. As Goudsblom (1970) shows, "high" systematically implies "better," "freer," and "stronger." Descriptively it would be more responsible and useful to identify language *varieties* and conceive of them sequentially in the order learned.

The purist approach might be characterized as a kind of cultural and linguistic imperialism, for it posits a single variety (of language or culture) as "correct" for all domains. Other varieties are felt to be in *competition*, with the one they seek to impart in the school. These other varieties are a "problem." Herndon (1969, 9) conveys the feeling of teachers toward such phenomena, noting that it is "something which happens all the time . . . but which isn't supposed to happen. A problem. You were supposed to believe in, and work toward, its non-existence." Rather than *adding* a linguistic variety to the child's repertoire (Gumperz, 1964a and 1964b; 1965; and 1969b and 1969c), it is felt that the school-approved "high" variety should *replace* the child's "low" variety. Steiner (1969, 212-15) refers to this as "de-education," i.e., the belief that the "lower-class" Mexican-American child "has to be de-educated before he can be re-educated," and adds that currently in the United States, "the de-education of La Raza is indeed overachieved."

Sociolinguistic factors underlie these pervasive purist beliefs. Labov (1971, 52) points out that "in a number of sociolinguistic studies it has been found that women are more sensitive to prestige forms than men—in formal style [. . .] and teachers in the early grades are women, largely from the lower middle class. This is the group which shows the most extreme form of linguistic insecurity, with the sharpest slope of style shifting."

[26] Labov (1971, 65) has affirmed that, "linguists [. . .] without a single dissenting voice [. . .] concur that this [cultural or verbal deprivation] is a superficial and erroneous interpretation of the very data presented in support of it." Nevertheless, this brutal term of sociocultural coercion has become very popular among educators. "Middle-class" ignorance of "lower-class" culture and language is rarely recognized. This is hardly surprising in view of the non-reciprocal power relations (see footnote 23 above) between the groups involved. To this one can add the ethnolinguistic fact (Wolff, 1964) that many teachers *will not,* and so *cannot* comprehend a linguistic or cultural variety which they hold to be "inferior" and "reprehensible." Hymes (1966, 34) has suggested the need for a conference on the "cultural deprivation" of "middle-class" teachers while noting its unlikelihood. Finally, economic deprivation is frequently (and conveniently) equated with "cultural deprivation."

The end result of these factors is a kind of "educational colonialism" with the "priests of education" busily "civilizing the savages."

The program is one-way with classes only for ethnic students. It is held that there is no reason for nonethnics to participate, or, if they do, that one must bend to the insufficient interest or ingrained prejudices of nonethnics and their parents.

The program, which lasts a maximum of three years, may begin with either the ethnic standard as a single medium, or with the ethnic and nonethnic standards as dual mediums of instruction. However, as rapidly as is pragmatically deemed possible, the time and treatment of the nonethnic standard is increased so that within a relatively short period of time the ethnic standard is used only for limited, nonessential subjects. Insofar as reading or writing skills in the ethnic standard are taught, it is the minimum considered necessary for establishing the base skills for their transfer to the nonethnic standard. Basically the developmental trend in all the program's features is towards rapid and near complete transfer to the nonethnic standard. The school's policy is essentially a "burnt bridges" approach: the ethnic language is seen only as a bridge to the nonethnic language— one to be crossed as rapidly as possible and then destroyed, at least as a legitimate medium of general instruction, although some voluntary classes in it as a foreign language may be maintained.

Apart from some early consideration of distant, ethnic-related culture,[27] the content of the curriculum emphasizes nonethnic, non-"lower class" interests and values. Ethnolinguistic matters are conspicuous by their absence and bilingual vocational counseling, if included, focuses upon traditionally stylized nonethnic characterizations of vocations, the exercise of which have been either antithetical or irrelevant to the existent culture of the ethnic majority, e.g., teaching, academic research, diplomacy, and positions with large supranational corporations.

Demonstration classes and public lectures may be held for ethnic parents in order to convince them of the value of the program and to interest them in an adult education program.

If an adult bilingual education program is offered, its structure is in most ways similar to the children's program. Its goal is functional literacy in the nonethnic standard via the ethnic standard if nec-

---

[27]Emphasis is thus on "symbolic ethnicity" rather than upon existentially persistent traditions. See also footnote 14 above.

essary. Almost all effort is focused upon English as a second language (ESL) component.

Extracurricular activities, whether recreational or more serious, for young or old or both, tend to radiate a "high" and distant, ethnic-related culture.

Evaluation of the assimilation program is primarily focused upon testing the *quality of individual performances within the school setting* on a host of skill, aptitude, and attitude measures. The bias is narrowly academic, linguistic, and psychological.[28]

Summarizing the essential dimensions of the assimilation program we see that:

1) Because originated from "above" by elites and administered in taken-for-granted, traditional ways by nonethnic and supraethnic interests and forces, this program is likely to discourage ethnic community organization among the large majority and to stifle open appraisal of intragroup and intergroup conflicts.

2) The teacher exemplifies the ability of elite members of dominant cultures to master and propagate a "superior" brand of ethnic culture and language.[29]

3) The linguistic and cultural content of the assimilation program is metaphorically a "vertically" articulated one implying power and

---

[28]Some examples in each area are: *academic;* frequency of disciplinary problems, absenteeism, dropout rates, and academic achievement scores in all subject areas, *linguistic;* word recall, translation, and sentence-completion performance measures as well as tests for phonological, morphological, and syntactic "interference," *psychological;* attitudinal, interest, and "intelligence" test scores, etc. "Interference" and "intelligence" merit being enclosed in quotation marks in the opinion of this writer because, although originally developed in social science as neutral terms, they have both come to be frequently *used* by the educational establishment as symbolic justifications for crude and iniquitous methods of social control.

[29]Because pupils may more easily identify with an ethnic teacher, they may be even more effective than nonethnic teachers in implanting in the pupils a sense of shame and inferiority with respect to the local varieties of ethnic language and culture. Steiner (1969, 176-77) quotes one barrio leader as observing, "no one is more frightened, smug, and conservative, and harder on our people, than the typical schoolteacher [. . .] who has escaped from the barrios in a two-car port and a king-sized bed." Thus, for many, social mobility is up-and-*out* of the barrio. One's distance from the barrio is signaled geographically (suburbia), culturally ("high" ethnic culture), and linguistically ("correct" Spanish). In view of this it should be clear that local control and ethnic teachers are in themselves no panacea of guarantee of a pluralistic program. See also footnote 25 above.

hegemony. It emphasizes the superiority or inferiority of different varieties of language and culture and encourages restricting use to correct forms of school-approved varieties in all domains of usage. This may be successful in alienating the student from the ethnic language and culture of his home and community if there are few or no extraschool domains where the careful "middle-class" standard ethnic variety is appropriate. Preexistent stereotypes on varieties of language and culture, their speakers and carriers, held by youth and adults in both groups are unaltered or reinforced by these and other measures such as newspaper articles which describe the bilingual program as bringing "cultural enrichment" and a literate standard language to the "culturally deprived" and illiterate.

Analysis

Which of these models do current bilingual programs approximate? To answer this question we now turn to the materials on bilingualism available through the Educational Resources Information Center (ERIC, 1969) of the U. S. Office of Education (USOE) in order to examine the available reports and weigh their relevant structural features in terms of the two polar models.

This procedure presents two problems. First this file contains a collection of reports on programs existing in 1969 but cannot be taken to constitute anything like a representative sample of all bilingual educational efforts. A second drawback in using these materials is that reports currently present great problems of comparability because there is no adherence to even a minimal set of reporting categories such as numbers of hours of instruction in each language, or materials taught in each language. In order to make such reports more useful for secondary analyses, the USOE should develop and sanction adherence to minimal reporting criteria such as the National Institutes of Mental Health has encouraged with its program of model reporting areas for mental health statistics. This is an urgen need. [30]

Nevertheless, in spite of these two methodological problems inherent in the data used here, the results of this secondary analysis

---

[30] Mackey (1970, 80-82) has proposed a useful questionnaire which is an important step in the needed direction.

reveal such an overwhelmingly clear and one-sided trend that we can assume it gives us a picture of what kinds of bilingual education programs are currently multiplying in the United States.

The finding is that *the great majority of bilingual programs (well over 80 percent closely approximate the extreme of the assimilation model,* while the remaining few are only moderately pluralistic.

Thus, in direct contradiction to the usual program's statement of goals, the structure of "typical" programs can be expected to foster not the maintenance but rather the accelerated demise of the ethnic mother tongue.

This is to say that in most cases the ethnic language is being exploited rather than cultivated—weaning the pupil away from his mother tongue through the transitional use of a variety of his mother tongue in what amounts to a kind of cultural and linguistic "counter-insurgency" policy on the part of the schools. A variety of the ethnic language is being used as a new means to an old end. The traditional policy of "Speak Only English" is amended to "We *Will* Speak Only English—just as soon as possible and even sooner and more completely, if we begin with a variety of the ethnic language rather than only English!"

In light of this, the benefits to the ethnic language and culture optimistically supposed by many to be somehow inherent in any bilingual education program become suspect as one realizes that some (and today most) types of bilingual programs may achieve much more effectively what the earlier monolingual policy could not do.

The appearance of bilingual programs does indeed represent a new policy, but as currently structured, most seem designed as a change from an earlier policy of simple repression to a more "modern" and sophisticated policy of linguistic counterinsurgency.

I do not suggest however that those directly involved in bilingual programs consciously intend these consequences; most are undoubtedly dedicated and well-intentioned.

The relevant issue today is not simply monolingual vs bilingual education, but more essentially what *social* goals will serve the needs of the *majority* of ethnic group members and what *integrated set* of program design features will effectively realize them. Currently most programs are patchwork affairs, each searching for some distinctive gimmick and focusing its rhetoric and design toward the individual pupil in isolation from his family, peers, neighborhood, and community.

If this evaluation seems harsh, it may be important to the reader to know that since the above analysis of the ERIC data and its conclusion that most bilingual programs strongly foster assimilation and language shift, three important studies reviewing an even larger number of programs, many of which were more recently initiated, have all come to a similar conclusion.

For example, Gaarder (1970) has analyzed the official USOE program descriptions of all seventy-six bilingual education projects federally funded in the first year of Title VII operation and polled all project directors. He notes that "the disparity between aims and means is enormous," adds that "only six aim eventually to provide bilingual schooling at all grade levels, 1-12," and concludes, " 'bilingual education' . . . can serve the ends of either [Anglo] ethnocentrism or cultural pluralism."

The same trend again become clearly evident as one reads the many program descriptions reproduced by John and Horner (1971, 15-100) and Andersson and Boyer (1970, vol. 2, 241-91). John and Horner (p. 187) conclude with a warning: "Educational innovations will remain of passing interest and little significance without the recognition that education is a social process. If the school remains alien to the values and needs of the community, if it is bureaucratically run, then the children will not receive the education they are entitled to, no matter what language they are taught in."

More recently Andersson (1971, 24-25), after noting a steady decline in the number of proposals for bilingual education programs received by the U. S. Office of Education (315 for 1970, 195 for 1971, and 150 for 1972), concludes that, "the obstacles to success are indeed formidable. Perhaps the greatest of these is the doubt in many communities that the maintenance of non-English languages is desirable."

Yet exactly this pervasive doubt that ethnic language maintenance is desirable might be an important reason for promoting more *assimilation* programs.

Again the more basic issue is, "*What type* of bilingual programs?"

All this is not even surprising when one considers that the assimilation program is essentially an expression of the present social structures of most United States communities with sizable ethnic populations. The school has always been an institution representative of the powerful community interest groups and their mainstream beliefs. The majority of Chicanos simply do not at present have either the sociopolitical power or the detailed and clear policy on language and culture necessary for their indigeneous varieties of language and culture to be recognized in an institution for social *control* such as the school, which in all societies is one of the traditional sites where the results of overt and covert sociopolitical and cultural conflicts are operationalized in what, in English, we somewhat euphemistically call "school policies," rather than "cultural politics."

The difference between "policies" and "politics" is no idle matter of just words, but a consequential distinction implying two completely different modes of distributing power. "Policies" are generally understood to represent decisions appropriately made by professionals—in this case educators, administrators, and researchers. "Politics," however, directly implies the appropriateness of rights of influence and control (not just "involvement") in the decision-making process for lay or nonprofessional constituencies, especially those most directly affected—in this case the parents and children of the ethnic majority within the Chicano community.

To the typical Southwestern nonethnic American, the pluralistic program for Chicanos must sound radical, for it seems to him to assume a host of factors which his social upbringing has taught him are absent. Where is the ethnic community ideology, interest, and consensus necessary for promoting an ethnic-based bilingualism and biculturalism? Where are there ethnics with the prerequisite basic training needed for recruitment into such a program? How can an "illiterate dialect" be considered appropriate for use in the school? What culture does a "culturally deprived" group have worthy of inclusion in an academic program? And many ethnic members, especially those of the elite, have adopted these same views, which makes even more understandable the tendency to propose only "high" cultural and linguistic varieties as acceptable for a program proposal.

Indeed the pluralistic program *is* one which in many ways runs against the tide and almost appears to present a dilemma.

If the assimilation program is an expression of the status quo social structures, the pluralistic program is an expression of planned social change, and its introduction itself presupposes some basic social changes in intraethnic ideologies and power relations.

Fishman and Lovas (1970, 215) have suggested that "bilingual education in the United States currently suffers from three serious lacks: a lack of funds (Title VII is pitifully starved), a lack of personnel (there is almost no optimally trained personnel in this field), and a lack of evaluative programs (curricula, material, methods)."

Realizing that these are real problems, let us nevertheless assume that more money, trained personnel, and evaluative programs *are* forthcoming in the future. Will this assure any change away from the community demise of the ethnic language?

This question lends greater weight to the principal concern of Fishman and Lovas, who emphasize that most needed is greater sociological understanding of the social consequences of bilingual programs.

While one cannot predict the types of bilingual education programs which are likely to appear should more funds, personnel, and materials become available, there would appear to be a strong possibility that the result will not be pluralistic programs. One possibility is of course the proliferation of more numerous assimilation programs.

However, some changes may also be expected. Because the progressive phasing out of the ethnic language as a medium of instruction, or what Mackey (1970) calls a "transfer" curriculum, clearly achieves language shift *within* the school domain, and because a program in which the ethnic language continues to have a role as a medium of instruction throughout the progressive grades (a "maintenance" curriculum) obviously realizes ethnic-language maintenance *within* the school domain, many influential proponents of bilingual education are coming to recognize the exploitation of the ethnic language inherent in the transfer curriculum and are advocating the institution of more maintenance curricula.

No sociological acumen is required to see this much.

However, if planners of new programs focus almost exclusively upon the "time and treatment" curriculum issue, the following may easily happen: one begins with what is essentially a near ideal-typical assimilation program (which includes a school transfer curriculum) and inserts in its place a maintenance curriculum while retaining all the other features of the model. Such a change would be from a transfer-assimilation to a maintenance-assimilation program.

To call it a maintenance-assimilation program implies a contradiction, namely, that while realizing ethnic language maintenance within the school, it simultaneously promotes ethnic language shift within the community.

Is such a result possible? I would hypothesize not only that it is, but that there are sociological reasons for expecting that in certain social contexts, a maintenance-assimilation program may be an even *more* potent, albeit less visible, instrument of linguistic counter-insurgency than the transfer-assimilation method.

A few reasons for such a possibility can be most concisely suggested by a schematic outline of postulates, assumptions, and hypotheses which, it is recognized, can only be confirmed or refuted by future empirical research. (It should be clear that in my opinion most of the following hypothetical consequences are considered undesirable.)

The basic question is, "What are the diachronic effects of the maintenance-assimilation program on the local community dominance configuration?"

Postulate 1: Significant types of language shift may remain veiled unless in addition to the distinction between the ethnic and the nonethnic languages, intraethnic language varieties are differentiated. For purposes of this discussion only two varieties will be distinguished: the informal local ethnic language variety (ELV_L) vs a supranational world (Gaarder, 1971) ethnic language variety (ELV_W).

Postulate 2: A speaker will view his stronger language in a more differentiated manner than he will his weaker language. That is, members of the ethnic speech community will be more aware of, and sensitive to differential competence in their command of distinct *intra*ethnic language varities than they will be to either their differential *inter*language (ethnic vs nonethnic), or nonethnic *intra*language competence. For example, a member of the ethnic majority who is confident in his command of an informal ethnic language variety may, when faced with a situation requiring "correct" usage (ELV_W), become painfully aware of his felt inability and therefore opt to switch into the variety of the nonethnic language which he commands, although, for a native speaker of the nonethnic language this variety may be felt to be far from formal. However, if fellow ethnic community members constitute his audience (see assumption 2 below), such an interlanguage switch may be accepted as "more formal" than an intraethnic language variety switch because they hold similar norms highly differentiating varieties of their mother tongue and stereotyping the second language.

Assumptions:

1. The maintenance-assimilation program emphasizes ELV_W exclusively, i.e., either excludes ELV_L from the classroom repertoire completely or only tolerates it passively, e.g., the teacher does not overtly chastise a child for using ELV_L but will never use it herself.

2. The ethnic community is vertically stratified into a large "lower-class" majority and a small "middle-class" minority. Both tend to be residentially segregated from each other and from the nonethnic population—the majority more so than the minority.

3. The ethnic majority has broad competence in ELV_L and very limited competence in ELV_W, while the ethnic minority has more competence in ELV_W than in ELV_L.

4. Subjectively both the ethnic majority and minority sharply distinguish ELV_L from ELV_W.

5. Most members of the ethnic majority uncritically accept the ethnic minority's cultural and linguistic norms and their ethnolinguistic beliefs which characterize ELV_L as "low" "inexpressive," "incorrect," etc., and the ELV_W as "high," "eloquent," "correct," etc.[31]

Hypothesis 1: The maintenance-assimilation program will tend to *increase the use of ELV_W* in those community domains which: a) play a secondary role in the ethnic majority's everyday communi-

---

[31] There is an impressive array of supporting evidence for assumptions 4 and 5. Only a few examples can be given here. Alvarez (1967) calls Spanish "calo" a "snarl language." See also Barker (1971) and footnote 16 above. Even Haugen (1962) has characterized a number of normative dialect forms as "pathological."

cation networks, b) fulfill formal and ceremonial functions, or c) tend to be governed by channel constraints or nonreciprocal rights firmly establishing one group as predominantly senders and another as predominantly receivers,[32] i.e., are domains which tend to be controlled by the minority elite and assign a passive-receptive role to the majority. Some examples of such domains would be the formal parts of festive, ceremonial, and political gatherings, and mass media such as radio, television, and newspapers.

Hypothesis 2: The maintenance-assimilation program will tend to *decrease the use of ELV_L* in those community domains which: a) play a primary role in the everyday communication networks of the ethnic majority, b) fulfill intimate, casual, and informal functions, or c) are governed by reciprocal rights of participants, so that all persons involved engage in the productive and receptive use of language which is mutually controlled by the partners to the speech event.

Hypothesis 3: The maintenance-assimilation program will tend to *decrease the overall use of ethnic language vis-à-vis the nonethnic language* due to the greater prevalence and salience of informal over formal domains in the everyday life space of the ethnic majority. To use a quasi "evolutionary" metaphor, this result would amount to a sort of social "selection" of a "higher" species of the ethnic language—relegated however to a near vestigial or marginal role in community interaction. Ethnic language use in the community is thus "purified" and "elevated" while simultaneously isolated from the core functional concerns of the majority, where it is replaced by the nonethnic language, which is more categorically approved without such fine or detailed distinctions between its various varieties as are made between those of the ethnic language as briefly sketched in Postulate 2 above. It is as if the ethnic language were gaining legitimacy through death and supporters of such a trend felt "better a noble death than an ignominious life," that is, better the more restricted use of a "high" variety than a wider use of a "low" one.

The above hypotheses focus upon the ethnic majority. What might be the consequences for the ethnic minority?

Hypothesis 4: If the above postulates, assumptions, and hypotheses are valid, the maintenance-assimiliation program might be

---

[32]These terms are taken from Hymes (1964) etic paradigm of speech events.

expected to *increase* the use of ELVW within the communication networks of the ethnic minority elite and increase their control over the ethnic majority in local affairs while at the same time increasing the ethnic minority's opportunities for social mobility beyond either local or ethnic boundaries. The ethnic minority elite would thus become more dominant over, while simultaneously less dependent upon and more divorced from the local ethnic majority. This might place them in a particularly advantaged position for being easily co-opted by supraethnic interests dedicated to a colonial policy of indirect rule and make more difficult any attempts on the part of the ethnic majority to form independent sources of power and influence.[33]

Summarizing this series of hypotheses, one might say that if the transfer-assimilation program represents the ethnocentric triumph of nonethnic over ethnic values and interests, then in a sense the maintenance-assimilation program may bespeak a sociocentric victory of the ethnic minority elite over the ethnic majority's interests and values.

However, all these hypotheses, which suggest currently unanticipated consequences, must be put to empirical test.

As research can generally only discover what it sets out to find, adequate empirical tests can only be constructed by persistently holding on to the fundamental question: "What are the *social* consequences of particular bilingual education strategies upon the changing patterns of *community* language *use*?" And as the four hypotheses above seek to make clear, even such studies are likely to cast a net too coarse to catch the most significant changes unless a finer net is spun which recognizes the internal heterogeneity of the ethnic community and differentiates between intraethnic language varieties, and their communicative roles, status, and consequences for intraethnic community social and political organization.

From the contradiction between current statements of goals for bilingual programs and their likely outcomes—given their present (and likely future) structures—it would appear that many if not most bilingual programs are being unintentionally, yet falsely represented

---

[33] A recent example of such attempts at the development of independent sources of power is the formation of a third political party in 1970 and 1971 in several Southwestern states.

to those most directly affected by them, that is the pupils and parents of the ethnic majority.

Conclusion

From this one can conclude that future sociolinguistic research in this field has not only a scholarly but also an urgent democratic need to fulfill. Only by developing our knowledge of the longer range social consequences which specific programs have in their particular, heterogeneous, and stratified community contexts, and by developing an awareness of the range of possible alternative bilingual education models, can the real conflicts always involved in such projects become more visible and the interest groupings affected have a basis for developing a more enlightened stand towards the introduction and development of desired programs.[34]

Postscript

From the perspective of the above analysis it is particularly significant that at the time of the writing of this amended version (September 1971), after numerous communications with the U.S. Office of Education and correspondence with Project BEST (in New York City), which is engaged in a systematic review of the approaches used in every evaluative research component attached to each federally funded bilingual program in the United States, it has been possible to determine that *currently there is not a single study planned to determine program effects upon community diglossia.*

Such a glaring absence presents a phenomenon which itself deserves detailed investigation and should attract persons interested in the sociology of science and knowledge.

---

[34]The emphasis of this essay has admittedly been critical. The reader should not lose sight of the fact that a few pluralistic programs do exist. Additionally, many powerfully assimilationistic programs are admittedly very effective in reducing disciplinary problems, dropout rates, and absenteeism as well as promoting higher levels of academic achievement. Also, a strictly Anglo-oriented "cost analysis" of assimilation programs should show them to be a "good investment" and even a "bargain:" i.e., that they are effective in keeping youth off the streets, out of juvenile hall (courts), and will result in fewer of them in the future appearing on welfare and unemployment rolls.

The point, however, is that these traditional school- and budget-oriented goals can be achieved while simultaneously threatening or destroying community diglossia and hence the future of the ethnic community as such.

Why does this notorious research lacuna exist? Will it persist? Certain factors seem to maintain it. Psychologists, educators, and linguists far outnumber sociolinguists in the education research establishment. Also, the laymen, teachers, and administrators promoting bilingual education programs have primarily been members of the ethnic minority elite and nonethnics who are generally uninterested in, or directly opposed to many of the characteristics of the pluralistic model presented here. Existing programs naturally have a built-in interest in testing themselves on measures where they are likely to show "success" and justify their expenditures in terms which will be persuasive and adequate for those who decide upon the continuation of programs and the allocation of funds. On the basis of current trends, one could conclude that for those who presently decide, community language maintenance in general and maintenance of the ethnic majority's cultural and linguistic varieties in particular is manifestly irrelevant or simply not considered desirable.

There are, nevertheless, some positive signs. Fishman (1966 and 1971) has developed, applied, and refined the diglossic approach in several studies of different ethnic groups in the United States. Several centers for the preparation of sociolinguists have been developed in recent years. Gaarder (1971) has drawn attention to the significance of the relations between intraethnic language varieties and recommended the importance of giving local varieties a place in the classroom repertoire. And finally, within the Mexican-American community itself new political movements, leaders, and ideas more concerned with the future of the ethnic majority are being developed which are beginning to critically reexamine those of the ethnic elite minority.

Only one thing is certain. Not only do we not know what the major *social* consequences of different types of bilingual education programs are, but unless current trends and research priorities are basically altered, we are not going to know either—until too late, when the consequences have already been wrought and become sufficiently massive so as to be evident to all. But the important questions will then be of only historical interest.

Would it not be shamefully irresponsible to wait for such a post-mortem?

REFERENCES

Alatis, J. E. (ed.) *Bilingualism and Language Contact: Anthropological, Linguistic, Psychological, and Sociological Aspects.* (Report of the Twenty-First Annual Round Table Meeting on Linguistics and Language Studies, Georgetown Monograph Series on Languages and Linguistics, No. 23). Washington, D.C.: Georgetown University Press, 1970.

Alvarez, G. R. "Calo: The 'Other' Spanish," *ETCC* (Journal of the International Society for General Semantics) 24:1 (1967), 7-13.

Andersson, Theodore "Bilingual Education: The American Experience," paper presented at a conference sponsored by the Ontario Institute for Studies in Education, Toronto, Canada, March 1971.

———, and Mildred Boyer. *Bilingual Schooling in the United States.* 2 vols., Washington, D.C.: USGPO, 1970.

Baratz, Joan, and Roger Shuy (eds.). *Teaching Black Children to Read.* Washington, D.C.: Center for Applied Linguistics, 1966.

Barker, Marie Esman. *Espanol para el bilingüe.* Skokie, Ill. National Textbook Company, 1971.

Dillard, J. L. "How to Tell the Bandits from the Good Guys, or What Dialect to Teach?" *The Florida FL Reporter* (Spring/Summer 1969), 84-85 and 162.

ERIC File on Bilingualism: A list of the materials in this file and information on how they may be ordered appears in *The Linguistic Reporter* (Center for Applied Linguistics, Washington D.C.) 11:3 (June 1969), 6-7.

Ferguson, C. A. "Diglossia" *Word,* 15 (1959), 325-40.

Fishman, Joshua A. *The Sociology of Language: An Interdisciplinary Social Science Approach to Sociolinguistics.* Rowley, Mass., Newbury House, 1972.

———, R. L. Cooper, Roxana Ma, et al. *Bilingualism in the Barrio.* (Language Sciences Series) Bloomington, Ind.: 1971.

———. "The Politics of Bilingual Education," in Alatis, op. cit., 1970, 47-58.

———, and John Lovas, "Bilingual Education in Sociolinguistic Perspective." *TESOL Quarterly* 4:3 (September, 1970).

———. "Bilingualism with and without Diglossia: Diglossia with and without Bilingualism. *Journal of Social Issues,* 23:2 (1967), 29-38.

———. *Language Loyalty in the United States.* The Hague: Mouton, 1966.

———. "Who Speaks What Language to Whom and When?" *Linguistique,* 2 (1965), 67-88.

Gaarder, A. Bruce, "Teaching Spanish in School and College to Native Speakers of Spanish." (A report commissioned by the Executive Council of the American Association of Teachers of Spanish and Portuguese) mimeo., 1971.

———. "The First Seventy-Six Bilingual Education Projects," in J. E. Alatis, op. cit., 1970, 163-78.

———. "Organization of the Bilingual Schools." *Journal of Social Issues,* 23:2 (1967), 110-20.

Goudsblom, Johan. "On High and Low in Society and in Sociology: A Semantic Approach to Social Stratification," a paper presented at the 7th World Congress of Sociology, Varna, Bulgaria, September 1970.

Grebler, Leo, Joan W. Moore, and Ralph C. Guzman et al. *The Mexican American People: The Nation's Second Largest Minority.* New York: Free Press, 1970.

Gumperz, J. J. "Verbal Strategies in Multilingual Communication," in J. E. Alatis, op. cit., 1970a, 129-47.
———. "Sociolinguistics and Communication in Small Groups," (Working Paper No. 23) Berkeley, Calif.: Language Behavior Research Laboratory, April 1970b.
———, and E. Hernandez. "Cognitive Aspects of Bilingual Communication," (Working Paper No. 28) Berkeley, Calif.: University of California Language Behavior Research Laboratory, December 1969a.
———. "Communication in Multilingual Societies," *Cognitive Anthropology.* Ed. S. A. Tyler. New York: Holt, 1969b, 435-49. .
———. "Theme." *The Description and Measurement of Bilingualism.* Ed. Louis Kelley. Toronto: University of Toronto Press, 1969c, 242-53.
———. "Linguistic Repertoires, Grammars and Second Language Instruction." In *Report of the Sixteenth Annual Round Table Meeting of Linguistics and Language Studies.* Ed. Charles W. Kriedler. Georgetown University Monograph Series on Languages and Linguistics, No. 18 Washington, D.C.: Georgetown University Press, 1965, 81-90.
———. "Linguistic and Social Interaction in Two Communities." *American Anthropologist,* 66:2 (1964a), 37-53.
———. "Hindi-Punjabi Code Switching in Delhi." *Proceedings of the International Congress of Linguistics.* Ed. Morris Halle. The Hague: Mouton, 1964b.
Haugen, Einar. "Schizoglossia and the Linguistic Norm." *Georgetown Monograph Series on Languages and Linguistics,* No. 15 Washington, D.C.: Georgetown University Press, 1962, 63-73.
Herndon, James. *The Way It Spozed to Be.* New York: Bantam, 1969.
Hymes, Dell. "On Communicative Competence," mimeo., 1966.
———. "Introduction: Toward Ethnographies of Communication." *American Anthropologist,* 66:6; Part 2 (December 1964), 1-34.
John, Vera P., and Vivian M. Horner. *Early Childhood Bilingual Education.* New York: MLA, 1971.
Kjolseth, Rolf, Nora Margadant, David Lopez, and Enrique and Carmen Lopez. *Chicano Talk.* In preparation.
Labov, William, "The Place of Linguistic Research in American Society." *Linguistics in the 1970's.* (Prepublication edition). Washington, D.C.: Center for Applied Linguistics, 1971, 41-70.
———. *The Social Stratification of English in New York City.* Washington, D.C.: Center for Applied Linguistics, 1966.
Landmann, Salcia. *Jiddisch: Abenteur einer Sprache.* 3. Auflage. Muenchen: Deutscher Taschenbuch Verlag, 1968.
Lewis, Louisa. "Culture and Social Interaction in the Classroom: An Ethnographic Report." Working Paper no. 38 Berkeley, Calif.: University of California Language Behavior Research Laboratory, November 1970.
Loyo, Gilberto. "Prologo." Manuel Gamio. *El Inmigrante mexicano: La Historia de su vida.* Mexico: Universidad Nacional Autonoma de Mexico, 1969, 5-80.
Mackey, William F. "A Typology of Bilingual Education." T. Andersson and M. Boyer, op. cit., 1970. II, 63-82.
Macnamara, John. "Bilingualism in the Modern World." *Journal of Social Issues,* 23:2 (1967), 1-7.
Rayfield, Jr. R. *The Languages of a Bilingual Community.* The Hague: Mouton, 1970.

Romano-V., Octavio Ignacio (ed.). *El Espejo/The Mirror: Selected Mexican-American Literature.* Berkeley, Calif.: Quinto Sol Publications, 1969.

Rosenthal, Robert, and Lenore Jacobson. *Pygmalion in the Classroom: Teacher Expectation and Pupils' Intellectural Development.* New York: Holt, 1968.

Schmidt-Rohr, George. *Mutter Sprache.* 2. Auflage. Jena: Eugen Diederichs Verlag, 1933.

Steiner, Stan. *La Raza: The Mexican Americans.* New York: Harper & Row, 1969.

Stern, H. H. (ed.). *Foreign Languages in Primary Education.* Hamburg: UNESCO Institute of Education, 1963.

Stewart, William. "On the Use of Negro Dialect in the Teaching of Reading." J. Baratz and R. Shuy, op. cit., 1969.

–––. "Urban Negro Speech: Sociolinguistic Factors Affecting English Teaching." *Social Dialects and Language Learning.* Ed. Roger Shuy. Champaign, Ill.: National Council of Teachers of English, 1965, 10-18.

United States Office of Education. "Manual for Project Applicants and Grantees: Programs Under Bilingual Education Act (Title VII, ESEA)," draft, March 20, 1970.

Wolff, Hans. "Intelligibility and Inter-Ethnic Attitudes." *Language in Culture and Society.* Ed. Dell Hymes. New York: Harper & Row, 1964, 440-45.

Section Three

Language Education in Practice

10. Teaching English to Speakers of Other Languages: Problems and Priorities

Mary Finocchiaro

A central task of the language education of minority children is to provide them with access to the general culture and economy by teaching them the standard language. Thus, in the United States, the teaching of English as a second language is a key component, the absolute minimum, in any program for minority children. In the last few years, the field has become well-established, with its own professional organization (TESOL, James E. Alatis, Executive Secretary, School of Languages and Linguistics, Georgetown University, Washington, D. C. 20007) and its own professional journal (*TESOL Quarterly*). Its full range and concerns are represented in the anthology edited by Harold B. Allen, *Teaching English as a Second Language* (New York: McGraw-Hill, 1966; a second edition is planned for 1972) and in Kenneth Croft, *Readings on English as a Second Language: For Teachers and Teacher-Trainees* (Cambridge, Mass.: Winthrop Publishers, Inc., 1972). In the following article, Mary Finocchiaro reviews the field and discusses its relation to bilingual education. Her qualifications for the task are unexcelled: she is professor of education at Hunter College, a past president of TESOL, and author of a number of books in the field including the basic methods text, *Teaching English as a Second Language* (New York: Harper & Row, 1969). The article appeared in a special issue of *The English Record* devoted to bilingual education; it is adapted from an address that Professor Finocchiaro gave at the first meeting of the New York State TESOL affiliate.

The most challenging problem facing schools in every sector of New York State today is that of determining how best to help linguistically handicapped youngsters learn English well enough to function in a regular school program with profit to themselves and to their peers. The school's responsibility does not end there, however.

Reprinted from *The English Record,* 21:4 (1971), 39-47, by permission of the author and the publishers.

While its primary goal—in cooperation with other social and educational agencies—may be that of helping learners become well-adjusted participating school and community members, it must also prepare the learners for their future roles as citizens, parents, and workers.

On the surface, this may seem like a simple task. In reality it is fraught with frustration and feelings of failure and fear on the part of concerned school personnel and community leaders. There exists an urgent need to view the situation more realistically than we have done in the past lest another generation of learners become school "dropouts" or "push-outs." In the following discussions I plan to concentrate on the elementary and secondary schools where problems are most acute. I shall not touch on programs for literate, motivated foreign students at the college level or those for adults— literate or illiterate—who are generally highly motivated.

Before discussing some of the factors that contribute to the retardation of a quick or easy solution to a complex, emotionally charged problem, I should like to take a few moments to recall and comment upon a few highlights of my own experience as an English as a Second Language teacher. You will thus realize that many of the factors impeding progress today have their roots in decades of inflexible dogma which has been allowed to go unquestioned by concerned teachers and parents; you will realize, too, that cultural and/or parent-school conflicts of fifty years ago find numerous parallels today.

When I started teaching English as a second language, the supervisor asked me to use the Basic English method. I remember receiving a poor teaching evaluation because I had had the temerity to teach the word "mirror" and I had compounded the felony by taking a pocket mirror out of my purse to use as a visual aid! When I was forced to translate Blood, Sweat, and Tears to "red water from the body," etc., I thought "there must be another way" and began searching for it. It took a lot of soul searching and trials and errors to realize, of course, that there *is not just one other way.*

Then came the period of the "mimicry and memorization" of long dialogues; of the priority of habit formation; and of thinking that meaning and vocabulary were secondary or even comparatively unimportant. The teaching emphasis was primarily on helping students learn the signals and develop habits of using the sounds and structural signals of English.

With the "New Key" enthusiasts of the late fifties, listening and speaking skills assumed priority and reading was deferred for *one hundred hours!* Teaching grammar rules was considered comparable to breaking one of the commandments; translation was not to be mentioned under any circumstances.

In the middle sixties, some scholars began to think that language acquisition had nothing to do with habit formation and that a cognitive-code theory of language acquisition should *replace* the habit formation theory. The late nineteen sixties found staunch supporters of either one *or* the other learning theory; of those who believed more in communication than in manipulation; of those who preferred a transformational generative grammatical analysis to a structural one. There is a proliferation of articles and books about renewed emphasis on meaning and about an *unstructured, free* choice of learning experiences on the part of learners because they possess their own built-in "capacities and strategies." The teacher has become the "facilitator" of learning rather than the "model" or "dispenser" of learning. She is the creator of a climate "in which learning can flourish." I could add countless new clichés but the result would be the same. Many conscientious teachers today are not only confused about their role, but they also continue to feel unhappy about having to select one school or the other of linguistics or psychology. Their major concern remains that of doing an effective job of teaching English to speakers of other languages.

I have oversimplified shamefully but the fact remains that despite the heat generated by the thousands of arguments, experiments, and claims, few people have been really happy about the outcomes of most of the programs in English as a second language. Despite carefully written "performance objectives," attention to "cultural immersion," "manipulation," and "communication goals," I think it is fair to say that there is widespread dissatisfaction with the results achieved in the past. Is it because we have not defined terms carefully or is it because we have accepted—without questioning—some of the "findings" of psychologists, sociologists, or "educators" related to learning and teaching? In my opinion, it is a little of both.

I think it is also fair to say that 99.9 percent of all teachers of English as a second language want to fulfill their responsibilities to learners in terms of helping them to communicate and to achieve their aspirations and of making them well-integrated, well-adjusted human beings. Teachers want to be responsive to the needs and goals of the communities which they serve.

What stands in the way of establishing programs of excellence? Where do the problems lie? Some stem from the attitudes of the pupils themselves, of their parents, and of some ill-informed teachers; some can be laid at the door of linguists, sociologists, anthropologists, who have either allowed distortions of their principles to continue to flourish uncorrected or, worse still, have published "research findings" based on inadequate experimentation. A large measure of responsibility for failure must also be ascribed to educators and supervisors who have found it "useful" to make statements which, while giving parents and community leaders false hopes, give conscientious teachers feelings of insecurity; to wit, a youngster (no matter at what age he was admitted to school) needed only a few weeks in the school—in a regular classroom—to become fully "integrated"; reading grades jumped four years after use of this or that piece of equipment or technique.

Important though they are, I shall not touch upon pupil and parent attitudes and motivation. I am convinced that a good English program which gives students the skills they need to become part of the mainstream of the school, which strengthens their assurance that what they are learning is useful to them *now* and not just at some vague future time, is intrinsically motivating. And it would be the unnatural parent who were not caught up in the enthusiasm engendered by the feeling of success and achievement which he notes in his offspring.

Allow me to examine briefly instead some of the labels or statements which have done learners and their teachers no little harm. As I mention them in random order, I shall also note some obvious implications. Let me start with those things in which *I do not believe.*

1. *I do not believe,* for example that any learner is "culturally deprived."

All human beings have culture. All youngsters come to school with two priceless assets—their native language and their culture. I do not even believe that people are as culturally "different" as some would have us think. Teachers, curriculum planners, and textbook writers should emphasize the universality of human values and should point out the role of geographical and historical factors in the development of cultural differences—if these do, in fact, exist.

2. *I do not believe* that children of low socioeconomic status come to school without language and without concepts. It may take a longer time for the language they know to be brought to the surface, but it can be done because *language is there.* Moreover, whether or not parents can "reinforce" the school's language activities, teachers still have the major responsibility for reviewing and "reentering" the English that has been taught as often as feasible in varied experiences which will require the use of utterances of increasing complexity.

3. *I do not believe* that English can be acquired by osmosis. Even very young children need systematic language development unless they live in a predominantly English-speaking community where they interact constantly with their English-speaking peers. The mere sitting in the same classroom with English-speaking children is generally valueless (as far as language acquisition is concerned) without a carefully planned language program in which all the features of English pronunciation, morphology, and syntax are presented and practiced intensively in activities appropriate to the maturity level of the learners.

4. *I do not believe* that the learner's growth will be stunted if—at an early age—and with a sympathetic, skilled teacher—he is encouraged and helped to use a "standard" English pronunciation and grammar. *The majority of parents want this for their children.*

5. *I do not feel* that the judicious use of the learner's native language—by the teacher, a paraprofessional or a student "buddy"—will have a harmful effect on him. The native language—used sparingly of course in ESL classes—will clarify needed directions or concepts, will orient the newcomer and more especially, will enable him to establish a more immediate rapport with some other human being in the strange classroom.

6. *I do not believe* that a contrastive analysis of English and the student's native language alone should determine the selection and gradation of the linguistic material to be taught. The items for initial presentation should not necessarily be those which contrast with those in the learner's native tongue. Not only may the learning of possible parallel features give him a greater feeling of security but there are, in addition, two other major considerations:

a) When English is taught as a *second* language; that is, for immediate use in the surrounding community, the items needed to help the learner function in the situation must be given priority.

b) Often the interference between the learner's native language and English may not be as serious as that caused by a partially learned feature of the English language and segments of the feature not yet presented or practiced. Learners often make false analogies because they try to apply partially or incompletely assimilated material to other contexts.

7. *I do not believe* that all teachers, particularly those in service for many years, should be required to learn the native language of their students, particularly when they teach English to more than one ethnic group. I think it would be most desirable if all teachers learned to use expressions of greeting and concern and some of the requests and formulas useful in facilitating classroom management. The learners would be the losers, however, if teachers were made to feel inadequate in their task of teaching English and if their morale were lowered by such an unrealistic demand.

I would urge, nonetheless, that teachers gain some knowledge not only of the broad features of pronunciation or grammar which will cause problems in their students' acquisition of English but also of possible cognates in the two languages.

Prospective teachers *can* be expected to study a foreign language intensively, particularly the dominant foreign language of the community in which they plan to teach. Colleges serving community schools have a grave responsibility in preservice training programs for teachers. They should introduce strong relevant courses in those foreign languages spoken by the minority groups in the community and should make these *required* courses for the bachelor's degree.

While we cannot expect teachers without previous extensive experience in foreign language to become bilingual enough to use the students' native language in teaching ESL or to teach curriculum areas in the students' native tongue, we should insist that *all* teachers become *bicultural*. It is imperative that all teachers of ESL gain a deep insight into the life styles and cultures of their learners, even when more than one ethnic group is involved.

8. *I do not believe* that learners should be required to speak about *English* culture only in English.

It would be a great source of pride for them if they could talk about their culture in the target language. Such a procedure would serve another valuable purpose: that of enabling learners to perceive that English can be an instrument of communication in just the same way as is their native tongue. The insistence on "cultural immersion" as it has been advocated up to now is totally unrealistic, ignoring, as it does, basic psychological principles of human learning.

9. *I do not believe* that units written for English language learners should concentrate primarily on aspects of slums or ghettos, where the non-English newcomers may be living temporarily. While I consider it important to start with children where they are in terms of ability, background, environment, etc., it is disheartening to see entire units in the English language devoted to vocabulary and concepts related to slum living. These might *occasionally* be used by a teacher whom learners consider empathetic as a point of departure for the introduction of language material. The emphasis in the curriculum (used in the broadest sense of the word) should be (a) making pupils and their parents aware that the learning of English may be one way of moving out of the slums; (b) giving them the skills and tools which are indispensable to further their education; and (3) initiating projects with other agencies in the community which can serve not only to improve conditions but also to enable learners to use English which is meaningful and relevant to them.

I also question the advisability of books for young children written in so-called Black English. To begin with, not all black children speak Black English! Moreover, I am not convinced that this intermediate step of reading in the second *dialect* before reading in the standard dialect is necessary. Much more experimentation and discussion with concerned parents is needed before teachers are allowed to make widespread use of such books in their classrooms. Not enough has been written and said about the time and manner of making the transition to the reading in the standard dialect. Furthermore, English dialect speakers understand "standard" English when spoken or read aloud. We should not confuse the learning problems of the non-English speaker and the dialect speaker although some teaching techniques may be similar for both groups.

10. *I do not believe* that group IQ tests should be used as a basis for placing learners into any level or grade of an English program. All

of us are aware that (a) most IQ tests are not culture free; (b) they do not test many of the facets of intelligence which should be included under the term of "general aptitude"; (c) they should be studied with all other factors or records concerning the learner; and (d) results are often interpreted incorrectly. In any case, in an English-speaking community, English *must* be taught to *all* normal pupils.

11. *I do not believe* that with the majority of learners above the ages of twelve or thirteen the ESL curriculum should require—as intermediate or terminal behavior—a mastery of all features of pronunciation. Any improvement in pronunciation at that age level will generally be gradual and not dramatic. The goal should be comprehensibility at all times but not necessarily allophonic perfection. With many learners, the inordinate amount of time spent on "drilling out" an accent which does not impede comprehension, could be more profitably used in other productive learning activities..

12. *I do not believe* that *functionally illiterate* students admitted to schools and placed with their age peers in the upper junior high schools or in the secondary schools can close the five-or-more-year gap without an intensive, specially designed program in English and in their native tongue.

And now let me turn to some facets of the ESL programs in which I have come to believe after several decades of teaching at all levels, observation of many classrooms, and talks with teachers, supervisors, and concerned parents.

Despite the extravagant claims made by some language schools, learning one's first language and one's second language are not the same. Every normal child learning his first language has an innate capacity for doing so, but in learning the new language such factors as age, the duration of the learning period, the opportunity for using the new language, linguistic interference, and attitudes require quite different approaches and techniques and may force schools to write quite different performance objectives as well as to modify terminal goals.

Professional leaders in our field and community resource persons must become increasingly aware of the fact that it is asking superhuman efforts of teachers to expect them to work with English-speaking children and language learners within the same classroom.

The former may be reading at different "grade" levels; the latter may be at various levels of literacy not only in their native tongue but also in English. Each learner will be at a different point on the continua of the English communication skills (listening with understanding, speaking, reading, and writing).

Homogeneous grouping of English language learners for intensive English instruction for a flexible period of time; with a teacher well-trained in teaching ESL; with specially designed instructional materials; and with continuous evaluation of the learners' progress *and* of the program is the only viable organizational pattern at the present time. Even in this pattern, I am assuming, of course, that the ESL learners will spend at least two hours each day with native English-speaking youngsters in art, music, physical education classes, and in other activities where a language deficiency is not a serious handicap.

Temporary homogeneous grouping which will accelerate the learners' admission to the regular school program should not be equated with segregation. I have seen ESL learners seated in classrooms with native English speakers but not involved in any way with the learning activities. That, in my mind, constitutes the worse kind of segregation.

"Pull-out" programs in which ESL learners come together from various classrooms for English instruction—unless carefully planned—do not provide long enough periods of intensive help; do not ensure continuity of instruction for the learners; and generally, do not make it possible for them to integrate the English they have learned in the special English class with that needed in the other curriculum areas.

Provision must be made for individualized instruction, but it is essential that boards of education and other agencies assist teachers in the herculean task of preparing material which will enable learners to acquire the essential features of English phonology, grammar, and lexicon and culture so that they can encode and decode language. While the material must be individualized according to need, blocks of material should be presented to the entire class whether the class is composed both of native and nonnative English speakers or of ESL learners alone. This is necessary if the learners are to be given the feeling that they are part of a group and that they are capable of sharing experiences with their peers.

Emphasis in teacher-education programs should be placed on the values of grouping and the techniques of group dynamics. Diagnosing individual pupil needs, identifying possible experiences to be shared, preparing materials and evaluating progress so that pupils can be moved in or out of groups as needed should all be included among the skills which a teacher should acquire.

The discrete items within the English program (pronunciation, grammar, vocabulary, cultural facts) should be presented and practiced within two major contexts: the everyday authentic situations needed for living in the community and, as quickly as possible thereafter or *concurrently,* the basic vocabulary, forms, and patterns required for effective participation in all the curriculum areas offered by the school for learners of that age level.

There should be no one inflexible approach or method for teaching English espoused by a teacher, school, education board, or community member. Since we do not really know how people learn, the approach should be eclectic and should make provision for the possible different learning styles of pupils. For example, reading should not be deferred for a specific number of hours. All the pupil factors of age, literacy, need, and motivation must be considered before determining the number of hours of possible deferment.

To illustrate further, grammar should be taught to pupils over the age of ten or eleven—not the traditional grammar rules, but generalizations based on numerous examples of the item being presented. It is näive of educators to keep discussing habit formation versus cognitive code theory. Both are necessary if students are to attain a desirable level of competence and performance in English.

Teachers should be permitted to discard or to modify techniques which they find basically counterproductive. To cite one example, asking students to memorize long dialogues without the further, judicious exploitation of the dialogue does not contribute enough to the growth of language ability and especially to the free, spontaneous use of English.

Colleges or other training agencies must help teachers acquire an understanding of and practice in: (1) helping students acquire reading skill at all levels; (2) adapting texts in all the curriculum areas for at least two or three levels of literacy; and (3) exploiting happenings and relevant school-community situations which, "discussed" in English, will be motivating to learners.

We should study more fully and apply to programs in the United States the comparatively unfamiliar concept of registers, which has gained currency in England and in many other countries. After a basic corpus of materials has been presented—adequate for functioning in the school and community—the language items selected for inclusion should depend, wherever possible, on the "felt" needs and aspirations of the learners. Since needs and aspirations change, however, learners must be taught how to learn so that they can continue their study of additional "registers" after leaving the school program.

After a thorough study of all the components which should be considered before instituting *any* program, a bilingual-bicultural program should be designed by all schools which will enable the ESL learner (1) to develop his native language not only for self-realization but also—with learners past primary school age—as a vehicle for learning basic concepts of living in the school and in the unfamiliar community; (2) to gain a deeper understanding of his cultural heritage as a source of pride and enhanced self-concept and as a means of accelerating his integration into the English culture; (3) to understand, speak, read, and write English well enough to communicate with his English-speaking neighbors; (4) to avail himself of all educational opportunities and to become part of the movement for upward mobility which our country offers.

Scholars in all areas related to the teaching and learning of ESL should be held accountable for specificity and clarity in reporting the results of their experimentation. Such factors as the numbers of persons involved in the experiment and the conditions under which it was performed should be carefully stated. Cautions or undesirable "side effects" should also be set forth. Too many educators or community leaders in the desire to be "innovative" rush to make use of the results of reported experiments without realizing that what may have worked with a small group or with one type of pupil population, with all the resources that are generally poured into an experiment, cannot be duplicated in their communities where the variables are not comparable.

Since a characteristic of many inmigrations is a high degree of mobility (due to such community factors as inadequate housing or poor vocational opportunities), leaders in the ESL field should cooperate in the preparation of a basic corpus of materials in English.

This would make possible better placement for the learner as well as continuity of instruction and it would facilitate the conscientious teacher's task who must know "where learners are." (A proficiency test—while valuable—would not serve the same purpose.) Needless repetition of learned material could be avoided when the need for newcomers is to move ahead as quickly as feasible. By the same token, the large gaps between what the teacher thinks the learner should know in grammar, etc. and what the learner has actually been taught would be lessened.

Two comments should be added: (1) The basic corpus would have to be supplemented or modified depending upon the ESL and school program to which the learner seeks admission; (2) Forms for reporting the points on the corpus which the learner had reached as well as the degree of competence and performance in each of the features or skills would also have to be devised cooperatively and disseminated on a nationwide basis.

Last but not least, while I am convinced that well-planned bilingual education programs should be expanded and that more efforts should be made within them to make native English speakers bilingual and bicultural, I should like to express other concerns. Some confusion seems to exist at the present time about the terminal goals of many programs; about the ESL component; about our obligation to other minority groups such as Turks, Poles, Italians, or French, who are coming to the United States in greater numbers.

If we believe honestly that bilingual programs have merit—and of course they do—and if we believe that every learner should have the benefit of equal educational opportunities, we cannot justify the exclusion of any groups.

Moreover, we should ask ourselves in this educational endeavor as in any other, questions such as, *Who is the learner we are considering?* (How old is he? How literate is he in his native tongue? How much previous schooling has he had?) What is the dominant language of the community? What human resources do we have to implement the program? What will be the role of teachers and of paraprofessionals? When do we start a bilingual education program? (For what age group, for example?) What curriculum areas should be studied in the learner's native language? Which in English? When will the transition be made from the dominant language to English in the curriculum areas? How do all the members of the community feel about the introduction of the program? How can we ensure that a strong English component will be introduced and maintained? (After all, the learner is living in an English-speaking community.) How can we make sure that the learner's native language will be developed to his greatest potential?

Numerous other questions come to mind. There is no one right answer to any question, but some answers may be considered undesirable because they have been borrowed from other communities without adaptation or, worse still, they have been born out of political expediency or community pressures.

In conclusion, let me talk briefly about the priorities mentioned in the title of this paper. Some are implicit in much of what I have said but I should like to single out four of them which in my judgment require immediate discussion and action:

1. The need for community orientation and involvement. For example, English-speaking parents will want to understand why in some classes some of their children may not have a full day's instruction with the teacher because she will have to spend time to teach English to language learners. Parents of language learners will want to understand why their children are (or are not) placed in special classes; what the grading system means; what opportunities their children will have to enter college, etc. etc.

2. The need for viable language-learning "centers" where English as a second language can be taught intensively. The centers can be within a school, within a community (children might have to be bussed to a community center), within an agency, but under board of education supervision. All the safeguards for the learners of continuous evaluation, special curriculum, opportunities for shared experiences with English-speakers, and others noted throughout this paper must be guaranteed.

3. The need for special programs for the older functional illiterate for whom the junior or senior high school may be the terminal point of instruction.

4. Most important, the need for colleges and other agencies to develop teachers and other personnel both at the preservice and in-service levels who possess the skills, knowledge, insights, and atti-

tudes required in teaching English as a second language. It must be obvious by now that:

Being a native English speaker is not enough.
Loving the children is not enough.
Knowing the structure of the English language is not enough.
Becoming familiar with methods of teaching ESL is not enough.

All of these qualifications are essential but, more, much more is needed to teach a group of human beings English as a second language.

Our responsibilities in this area are grave and, as can be noted, multifaceted. The best thinking of many persons of good will *working together* is needed if the non-English speakers in our midst are to become bilingual and bicultural. For persons living in an English-speaking community, a command of English is still the key to personal-social adjustment, to integration, and to upward mobility.

We cannot afford to lose another generation of children. More than ever, our nation needs all its human resources functioning at top capacity. Teachers of English as a second language have a crucial role to play in helping our country to achieve its goal, and more important, in enabling the tapestry which is America to become enriched and more colorful by the contributions which newcomers can, and will make to it, if given the opportunities.

11. Educational Considerations for Teaching Standard English to Negro Children

Joan C. Baratz

When we talk about the language education of minority children, we must remember it involves not just those who speak a language other than English, but also those whose dialect is different from standard. There has been considerable debate about the special problem of Black speakers of nonstandard English. There are two major questions: how different is their language, and to what extent might the principles or practices developed in teaching English to speakers of other languages be used with speakers of other dialects? In the following paper, Dr. Joan Baratz of the Education Study Center, Washington, D.C., discusses these and related issues. Another version of this paper appeared under the title "Who Should Do What to Whom . . . and Why?" in *Linguistic-Cultural Differences and American Education*, a special anthology issue of *The Florida FL Reporter* (7:1 [1969], pp. 75-77 and 158-59); the whole issue can be highly recommended for further readings in the topics covered in this book.

It is commonplace to observe that lower-class Negro school children do not speak like white children — lower or middle class. Although there is considerable agreement on this empirical observation, there is a great deal of discussion and debate concerning its source, significance, and consequence.

Reprinted from *Teaching Standard English in the Inner City* ed. Ralph W. Fasold and Roger W. Shuy (Washington, D.C.: Center for Applied Linguistics, 1970), pp 20-40, by permission of the author and the publishers.

The Difference-Deficit Question

The systematic research on the language of lower-class Negro children has produced two general conceptual vantages concerning their verbal abilities. One camp, composed generally of psychologists and educators, has tended to view the language of black children as defective, i.e., the language of Negro children is underdeveloped or restricted in some way. These experimenters attribute the deficit to environmental factors, frequently observing that the mother doesn't interact with the child enough, doesn't read books to him, etc. The other camp, composed mainly of linguists, has viewed the language of lower-class Negro children as a different yet highly structured, highly developed system.

For several years these two "camps" operated quite independently — psychologists went along describing deficiencies while linguists went about detailing differences. Recently, however, with the advent of interdisciplinary programs, each group has developed an increased awareness of the other's position.

The question then arises whether a *deficit model* and a *difference model* can coexist. Can a language be a fully developed, complex system (according to the linguists) and yet still be deficient — insofar as it produces speakers with language and cognitive deficits (according to certain psychologists)? Or to put it another way, can these children have speech and language problems that affect interpersonal and intrapersonal communication that are not related to the dialect? Aside from about 5 percent of lower-class Negro children who along with 5 percent of the other populations of children, have speech and language deficits due to neurophysiological or psychological difficulties, it is not possible to generally characterize the speech of lower-class children as deficient.

Those psychologists who wish to believe that there is such a thing as a fully developed different system that produces cognitive deficiency rely heavily on the writings of Basil Bernstein, while not always showing that they clearly understand his work. Bernstein speaks of the language of lower-class speakers as a "restricted code" as opposed to the "elaborated code" available to the middle class. For Bernstein, this distinction seems to refer to language use, with no clear indication that speakers limited to restricted code suffer any cognitive deficit; it is only that their orientation toward the verbal channel will be different from that of elaborated-code speak-ers.[1] Many followers of Bernstein, however, have confused superficial forms with specific processes. If a form is missing in Negro non-standard, it is assumed that the process is absent as well. To show the fallacy of this, one need only point out that in Negro nonstandard the conceptual scheme "if" is, under certain conditions, used with-out any overt representation of the form "if." Thus while in standard English one might say "I don't know *if Robert can* come over to-night", in Negro nonstandard the equivalent would be "I don't know *can Robert* come over tonight." In the standard English version a vocabulary item is used to fulfill the interrogative function; in Negro nonstandard a structural shift is used. Nevertheless, both sentences (standard English and Negro nonstandard) are equally capable of conveying the questionableness of Robert's availability in the evening.

The researchers who concerned themselves with applying the re-stricted and elaborated code thesis to explanations of cognitive impairment in young black children not only relied heavily on superficial structural differences in language production (whose relationship to cognition is not clear), but also these same researchers failed to deal with the sociocultural variable and the role it might play in speech elicitation. For example, the task, "describe this pic-ture," may be perceived differently by different groups in different

---

[1] B. Bernstein, "Social Class, Linguistic Codes and Grammatical Elements," *Language and Speech,* 5 (1962), 221-40. Studies have proliferated from Bernstein's writings that take his assumptions and hypotheses concerning language and categorically turn them into a taxonomy of lower-class speech. For example, studies that show greater use of pronouns in lower-class than in middle-class speech have been erroneously interpreted to indicate greater abstraction on the part of middle-class speakers. On the contrary, there is no research to indicate saying "The big red fire engine drove through the street," is any more abstract than saying "It drove through the street." Speech style is being confused with (and substituted for) language abstraction. Bereiter perhaps is most glaring in his "bastardization" of Bernstein when he suggests that if the child "does not know the word *not* . . . he is deprived of one of the most powerful tools of our language." (C. E. Bereiter, "Academic Instruction and Preschool Children," in R. Corbin and M. Crosby, eds. *Language Programs for the Disadvantaged* (Champaign, Ill.: National Council of Teachers of English 1965).) Although the Negro child does not use *not* – i.e., "this is not a book." he does use "ain't no" – i.e., "that ain't no book" which is no less powerfully logical!

settings. Mexican peasants, when given a picture of people engaged in an activity, are likely to "describe the picture" by detailing personality factors like "she's sad," whereas lower-class English boys may be more likely to describe the action that the individuals are engaged in — "he's throwing him the ball." Middle-class white Americans may feel that "to describe a picture" is to elaborate on all the details of a picture — i.e., setting, action, and feelings. This does not mean, of course, that Mexican peasants are incapable of responding to pictures by detailing the setting or the actions that are taking place. One need only define the task as such, i.e., "tell me what is happening in this picture," rather than "describe the picture."

Erickson[2] has illustrated that black children use both restricted and elaborated codes — the frequency of either code being determined by the subject matter, the setting, and to whom the individual is speaking. He has demonstrated the futility of presuming that black children do not use elaborated codes.

Perhaps of more importance than the demonstration that black children use both elaborated and restricted codes is the evidence most clearly demonstrated by Labov that one can produce highly abstract concepts while using extremely "restricted" codes.

A black teen-ager was asked, "Just suppose there is a God; would he be white or black?" When he responded "He'd be white," the interviewer asked "Why?" "Why? I'll tell you why. Cause the average whitey out here got everything, you dig? And the nigger ain't got shit, y'know y'unerstan'? So-um-for-in order for that to happen, you know it ain't no black God that's doin' that bullshit." The code the teen-ager has used is clearly nonstandard and, in terms of the Bernstein classification system, can be viewed as "restricted." Nonetheless in terms of logic and complexity it is no less restricted than the elaborated standard English equivalent "I know that God isn't black, because if he were, he wouldn't have arranged the world the way it is."[3]

---

[2] Fredrick Erikson, "F'get You Honky!: A New Look at Black Dialect in School," *Elementary English,* 46: 4 (1969), 495-99.

[3] Taken from W. Labov, "The Logic of Nonstandard English," *The Florida FL Reporter,* Spring 1969, 60-74, 169. Also printed in Alatis, J. (ed.), *Monograph Series on Languages and Linguistics (20th Annual Roundtable Meeting),* Washington, D.C.: Georgetown University Press, 1969), 1-45. For a discussion of the problems of employing a deficit model see Baratz and Baratz, "Early

Those researchers who would feel that language styles can be hier-archically distributed with more elaborated codes indicating more complex thought will first have to deal with the matter of equiva-lences across codes. The absence of such discussions in the literature, along with the fact that there has been little demonstration that the presence of certain linguistic forms and usages impair cognitive abil-ity makes it quite clear that the deficit model cannot be applied in relation to cognitive ability and language style.

Indeed, the fact that the language structure and style is different in the black community from that of the white mainstream serves only to indicate that the tests that black children are given initially cannot be used as measurements of potential so much as evidence of what black children know about the mainstream culture. Their poor performance by white mainstream standards merely indicates that they must be taught how to negotiate in a cultural setting that is different from their own.

Nonetheless, the differences in language structure and usage can be handicapping to the nonstandard speaker when he is expected to operate in a system that demands the use of standard English struc-ture and style. This language difference will create a problem in terms of oral communication in standard English settings. But the scope is even broader. His success in school programs may be hinder-ed because interference from his different linguistic system can cause difficulties in his learning to read and write standard English, the lingua franca of the public schools.

Is It Necessary for Black Children to Learn Standard English?

Given the fact that many black children do not speak standard English upon entering school (and quite frequently still do not speak it when leaving school), the question is raised: What should the school system do about this situation? Should the school system require that these children learn standard English?

Childhood Intervention: The Social Science Basis of Institutional Racism," *Harvard Educational Review,* Winter, 1970.

There are those voices in the academic community who say no, standard English need not be taught to these children.[4] These critics rightly feel that the child's language system is a fully developed, totally adequate linguistic system which is no better or worse than standard English and therefore, they think, it should be accepted as a perfectly adequate substitute standard English.

Nevertheless, there are several fallacies, overt and implied, in the argument against teaching standard English to black children. First, although it is true from a linguistic viewpoint that all dialects (Negro nonstandard, Standard American English, Oxford English, etc.) are equal, it is also true from a social viewpoint that some dialects are considered more valuable than others in certain contexts. The linguistic relativity, then, does not take into account the social reality. Middle-class individuals still rate Standard American English as more desirable than Negro speech. Pejorative ratings are associated with Negro nonstandard speech despite its viability, complexity, and communicativeness as a linguistic system.[5]

Indeed, despite the fact that various dialects may be used orally, the exigencies of reading and writing call for standard English and there are virtually no voices in the black community calling for newspapers and textbooks, to say nothing of carpenters' manuals, written in Black English.

The existence of standard English is not the result of a political conspiracy "to keep the black man down," but rather standardiza-

[4]Wayne O'Neil ("Paul Roberts' Rules of Order: The Misuse of Linguistics in the Classroom," *The Urban Review,* 2: 7 [1968], pp. 12, 17) insists that "instead of 'enriching' the lives of urban children by plugging them into a 'second' dialect . . . we should be working to eradicate the language prejudice, the language mythology, that people grew into holding and believing." Although I agree with Mr. O'Neil that something should be done concerning misconceptions about language in the educational establishment, I do not feel that this should be done *instead* of second-dialect teaching but rather in addition to the second-dialect training for Negro ghetto children. Learning the mainstream tongue is as important for the black child as is eradicating the misconceptions in *both* the white and black community concerning this original dialect.

[5]The pejorative ratings of Negro nonstandard English by most blacks is a factor which must be taken into account here. Negro self-hate is perhaps a more potent force today than white oppression, in the denial of the worth of Negro dialect. For more information on attitudes toward Negro nonstandard speech see Roger W. Shuy, Joan C. Baratz, and Walter A. Wolfram, "Sociolinguistic Factors in Speech Identification" — Final report, MH15048-01, NIMH, 1969.

tion is a sociolinguistic fact of life. Societies are socially stratified – whether the organization is a clan, a tribe, or a nation-state. It would be nice to think that there are complex, socially stratified societies where the spectrum of standard language is so broad as to include all the different grammars and usages of persons speaking the many varieties of that language under the label of "standard." Sad to say, human behavior just doesn't operate like that. To date, wherever research has been done – in Europe, Asia, and Africa – this has not been the case. One variety of the language invariably becomes the standard – the variety that has grammar books written in it, the one for which an orthography is established, the one that is studied by the populace in school. Language standardization appears to be a universal aspect of language variation in a national context – particularly one involving literacy. There is standard English, standard Arabic, standard Yoruba, and standard Hausa, just to note a few. Standardization is not a political invention of racist whites to exploit the Negro, rob him of his heritage, and denigrate his language.

The second fallacy of the "don't teach standard English" argument is the implication that in the process of learning standard English, the black child will necessarily be taught to devalue his "native tongue" – nonstandard vernacular. There is no reason to assume that a child cannot learn several dialects of English, and where it is appropriate to use them, without weakening his self-confidence, self-identity, and racial pride.

Another problem with such an argument is that it overlooks the point that in refusing to teach standard English to these children we cut off even further their possibility of entering the mainstream of American life.[6]

And finally, not teaching the black inner-city child standard English not only further hinders his ability to ultimately compete in

---

[6] I do not wish to suggest that the use of standard English by black children will insure their success in middle-class white America or that it will erase prejudice against Negroes, nevertheless, since standard English is the language of the mainstream it seems clear that knowledge of the mainstream system increases the likelihood of success in the mainstream culture.

the mainstream of society in terms of oral skills, but also makes the child's task of learning to read considerably more difficult.[7]

It seems clear from the discussion above that it is necessary to teach standard English to nonstandard speakers. They must know the language of the country if they are to become a part of the mainstream of that society. The need for teaching standard English to these children, however, does not rule out the use of nonstandard English within the classroom. It does not contradict the call for new, more meaningful curricula for these children, nor does it exonerate past failures on the part of the school system. It simply reaffirms the goal of the school system to turn out literate citizens who can compete in and contribute to the mainstream culture. In order to do this the school must teach all children the language of the mainstream.

Who Should Teach Standard English to Black Children?

Once it is determined that it is necessary to teach black children standard English, the question arises who should do this. Who in the school system is prepared to deal with this problem? At the present time there is no individual department in the school system that can deal with it.

Some English teachers, despite their previous training towards conceptualizing standard English as right and "God-given" and all other dialects as wrong and bad, have begun to take an interest in the issue of training Negro nonstandard speakers. Some speech teachers, despite their previous tradition of looking at deviance from standard language as pathology, have begun to express concern over helping black children learn to speak standard English. Some foreign language teachers with their background in comparative linguistics have also become interested in dealing with the problem of "second-language learning" as it applies to black children learning to speak standard English. It is my feeling that from this cadre of interested

---

[7] Study after study has demonstrated that children with a different language system from that of the national language have a great deal of difficulty learning to read when taught to read in the national tongue (UNESCO Conference on World Literacy, 1953). The Negro nonstandard speaker trying to learn to read with a standard English text is in much the same position as children learning to read a language other than the one they speak. For further discussion of this issue see J. Baratz, and R. Shuy, *Teaching Black Children to Read,* (Washington, D.C.: 1969), Center for Applied Linguistics.

individuals with their varied backgrounds a specialist can emerge who will be effective in coping with the language problems of ghetto youngsters. Such an interested person, however, must be well trained. High motivation and a dedicated soul are not substitutes for competence when it comes to teaching children.

One of the first issues to be dealt with concerning the teacher is the question: Should the teacher who wishes to teach black children be black?

Many black nationalists have been insisting that the teachers of black children be black. What these same nationalists have scrupulously avoided discussing is the fact that many middle-class Negroes (from which, of course, the majority of black teachers continue to be drawn) are as antighetto black as the white teachers. They share the white teachers' ignorance and prejudice toward the black child and his language.[8] They are careful to proclaim that they never spoke dialect.[9] They, too, believe all the current dogma and mythology concerning the child's homelife and its consequent effect on his learning. A black teacher may surely be helpful to these children in terms of the teacher's own experience as a black person, but that in itself does not provide any assurance that the child will learn simply because the teacher is the same color as he (surely the failure of the black school system is a testament in part to that fact). Just as high motivation and good intent are not enough, black skin per se does not insure effective teaching of black children – competence, which is colorless, is a necessary ingredient for success.

Developing an Urban Language Specialist

1. *The need for a specialist.* What does the teacher of black children have to know? How is she to be trained?

---

[8] It was a Negro, Charles Hurst, Jr., who coined the now disreputable term "dialectolalia" which he defined as an abnormal speech pattern characterized by "oral aberrations such as phonemic and sub-phonemic replacements, segmental phonemes, phonemic distortions, defective syntax, misarticulations, limited and poor vocabulary, and faulty phonology. These variables exist commonly in unsystematic multifarious combinations." (Charles Hurst, *Psychological Correlates in Dialectolalia,* Cooperative Research Project No. 2610, Communications Sciences and Research Center, Howard University, 1965.)

[9] At a recent talk on Negro nonstandard, I noticed two Negro teachers who stood in the doorway and assured all departing whites that "they always spoke this way" (in standard English).

First, a teacher who wishes to work with language and speech programs for black children must receive training concerning language. What is language? What are dialects? How do social factors influence language and language learning? What are the functions of a language? What is the relationship of spoken language to written language and reading? What is linguistic interference?

Second, she needs specific training in learning the child's vernacular. What is his language like? More specifically she should learn the dialect.[10] In the process of learning the dialect, I believe that the teacher will develop a greater respect for what it is she is asking of her children and what the difficulties are in learning another system, especially one which in many ways is superficially comparable to standard English. In addition, in learning the nonstandard dialect, the teacher will understand that one can learn another dialect of English without "changing" or "improving" the dialect that one already speaks.

Those teachers who already know the dialect will also need some of this training so that they can reorient their notion about Negro dialect, and can specify the areas where interference from the dialect will affect performance in standard English. Thus they will be able to anticipate problems as well as prepare lessons for teaching standard English.

Teachers will also have to learn something of foreign-language teaching techniques to aid them in preparing materials for presentation to children, and some of the evaluation procedures of speech therapy (with specific adaptations in reference to dialect speakers) to help them in assessing their effectiveness and the children's progress. Training of these teachers must also include discussions of the language arts curriculum, so that their new knowledge can be applied to making changes in materials and presentations that will aid in teaching reading and writing skills.

Lastly, these inner-city teachers must be familiar with the ghetto culture in addition to its distinctive language patterns. In talking about familiarity with ghetto culture one must be careful not to confuse psychological and sociological data with its emphasis on

---

[10] Learning a foreign language is not the same as learning a second dialect. The literature in verbal learning has indicated again and again that it is harder to learn material that is quite familiar than it is to learn two sets of distinct material.

normative behavior for ethnological fact. For example, the socio-logical fact that there is quite often no "man in the house" does not give us much information concerning what a ghetto family really is like. Perhaps the best example of confusing psychological data (inter-preted on the basis of a false premise-deficit thesis) for reality is the history of the professional conceptualization of the ghetto child's linguistic competence.[11] Since most people take the psychological data at face value, they presume that ghetto black children are verb-ally destitute and are truly amazed when they discover that verbal ability is highly regarded in the ghetto; ability to "sound" is im-portant and that the man of words is given considerable status by his compatriots.[12] Black children in elementary school are busy becoming proficient in the various toasts and in playing the dozens[13] even if they are all but mute when it comes to dealing with standard English situations in the classroom. The teacher must be aware of the different learning styles of ghetto youth and how they may affect the way material should be presented.[14]

Obviously the teacher who is to work in the black inner-city schools, and who is to institute new curricula with teaching styles suited for black children will have to be provided with a training program which incorporates the content described above. Such a specialist with this kind of training is sorely needed.

2. *Programs and materials available.* Granting that it is necessary for a specialist to teach standard English to nonstandard speakers, and given the fact that from various disciplines an individual can be

[11]See J. Baratz, "The Language of the Economically Disadvantaged Child: A Perspective," *ASHA,* 1968, and "Language and Cognitive Assessment of Negro Children: Assumptions and Research Needs," *ASHA,* 1969.

[12]See for example, Ulf Hannerz's Walking My Walk and Talking My Talk," in U. Hannerz, *Soulside: Inquiries into Ghetto Culture and Community* (New York: Columbia University Press, 1969).

[13]Playing the dozens, joining, sounding, rapping are terms for distinct verbal styles in the ghetto. For more information see R. Abrahams, *Deep Down in the Jungle* (Hatboro, Pa.: Folklore Associates, 1964); T. Kochman, "'Rapping' in the Black Ghetto," *Transaction,* 1969, pp. 26-34; W. Labov et al., "A Study of the Nonstandard English of Negro and Puerto Rican Speakers in New York City," Cooperative Research Project No. 3288, Volume II, *The Use of Language in the Speech Community,* Columbia University, 1968. .

[14]Some excellent beginning work on differences in cognitive styles in different ethnic groups can be found in G. Lesser and S. Stodolsky, "Learning Patterns in the Disadvantaged, *Harvard Educational Review,* 37: 4 (1967).

trained to work with these children, what kind of program should be instituted? What does the trained specialist do? First let us look generally at what has been done in the past and then discuss what needs to be done, and what the problems are that must be overcome in order to do the job well.

Speech and language programs have been devised that focused on the language abilities of preschoolers, elementary and secondary students, dropouts, and adult "new careers" people.

The preschool programs are best represented by the intervention programs known generally as "head start." The programs were developed on a deficit model, and most program directors believed that they were teaching these children language (not a second language). These programs were generally of two types:

a. Enrichment – here it was presumed that the language of the black child was underdeveloped due to lack of stimulation, poor mothering, etc., and the program was designed to compensate for this. The children learned about neighborhood workers, the friendly policeman, colors, nursery rhymes, etc. The best of the middle-class nursery school was presented to these children.

b. Academic – the now famous Bereiter and Engelmann[15] approach. These intervention programs were not based on underdevelopment of skills but rather on a presumed absence of the skills. These programs attempted to teach the children language arts[16] and mathematic skills through formalized instruction.

Since one of the avowed purposes of these early childhood intervention programs was to "improve language skills" (tacitly defined in these programs as teaching the child to speak standard English), one would have to say the programs were a failure in that there are no data to indicate that following a preschool intervention program, these children were more proficient speakers of standard English.[17]

[15]C. Bereiter and S. Engelmann, *Teaching Disadvantaged Children in the Preschool*, (Englewood Cliffs, N.J.: Prentice-Hall, 1967).

[16]Language arts involved formal instruction in the authors' concept of oral standard English and in beginning reading.

[17]Almost all of the data presented to date (see for example, Klaus and Gray, "The Early Training Project for Disadvantaged Children: A Report after Five Years," *Monograph of the Society for Research in Child Development*, 33, 1968) involve shifts (and transitory at that since they do not appear to be sustained once the child enters school) in IQ scores.

Despite the failure of these preschool programs to improve the black child's command of standard English, due largely to a lack of knowledge of what language is and how children learn language, the question still remains as to whether a child can be taught standard English as a "quasi-foreign language" at the preschool level. With adequately trained teachers and special materials perhaps the question of the optimal period for teaching these children standard English can be discerned. However, the optimal period for teaching children a second dialect still remains to be determined.

The junior high and high school programs have generally been zeroed in on as "prime times" to teach standard English as a second language to black children. The problem with many of these programs is that they use the jargon of second-language teaching but actually have as their goal the replacement of what they consider a substandard system (Negro nonstandard English which they give credence to as a legitimate system but to which they assign secondary status) with standard English.[18]

A prototype of such a program is Ruth Golden's "Improving Patterns of Language Usage." Although Mrs. Golden asserts that Negroes in low socioeconomic classes use nonstandard language patterns, she goes on to say that these patterns are "antiquated and awkward in structure." Further, she indicates that Negro nonstandard English is inferior since the "level of language [Negro nonstandard English] which has served very well for their parents is inadequate for them [Negro students]."[19] Despite the fact that she says the language patterns of Negro students ought not be solely those of the Negro community (implying more than one system), she actually feels that they should be solely standard English speakers as evidenced by her disappointment that " . . . many students who can speak well in class are not sufficiently motivated to continue in an acceptable [to her] informal pattern, but often revert to substandard

---

18See for example Ruth Golden's *Improving Patterns of Language Usage,* (Detroit: Wayne State University Press, 1960) or Virginia French Allen, "Learning a Second Dialect Is Not Learning Another Language," *Monograph Series on Languages and Linguistics, 20th Annual Roundtable Meeting,* (Washington, D.C.: Georgetown University Press, 1969), 189-202, where despite using second-language learning analogy Mrs. Allen concludes with an anecdote concerning the fact that the child is "worth revising."

19R. Golden, *Improving Patterns of Language Usage,* (Detroit: Wayne State University Press, 1960).

as soon as they leave the classroom." Her misinterpretation of the students' appropriate use of two language systems (standard English for the classroom and Negro nonstandard English for the peer group) as "insufficient motivation for using standard English" clearly indicates that her program is one of eradication of old patterns and replacement with acceptable patterns.

Mrs. Golden's programs as with most of the programs, teaching English as a second language to Negro nonstandard English speakers, relies on pattern practice as the *modus operandi* for acquiring standard English. The programs generally do not use contrastive techniques but rather rely simply on repetition of standard English patterns.

Nevertheless, programs have been initiated that genuinely respect the language of the student and that attempt to teach standard English using contrastive techniques.[20] The materials developed at the Center for Applied Linguistics provide one example of such a program.[21] This program not only implicitly recognizes the legitimacy of the students' system, but also uses both standard and nonstandard constructions in instruction and drill techniques. With such a teaching system, the student learns not only what standard English is but also how and where it differs from nonstandard English.

This technique is extremely important when dealing with teaching English as a "quasi-foreign language" and serves to underline one of the main differences between second-language teaching and second-dialect teaching. In second-language teaching the language to be learned is distinct enough from the students' own system so that he knows, for example, he is speaking French, whether well or poorly, and not English. In second-dialect learning this is not always so and in many instances the student does not know where nonstandard English leaves off and standard English begins. Therefore he quite often may not be sure, unless he is specifically

---

[20]See for example M. Gladney and L. Leaverton, "A Model for Teaching Standard English to Nonstandard English Speakers," *AERA* paper, 1968, for contrastive approach with young children or K. Johnson, "An Evaluation of Second Language Techniques for Teaching Standard English to Negro Students," *NCTE* paper, 1968, for use with older students.

[21]The materials, *English Now,* developed by Irwin Feigenbaum are currently being published by New Century.

instructed, when he is using standard English and when he is using forms that appear to be standard English. For example, in Negro nonstandard English *he working* would mean that he is working right now, whereas *he be working* means he is working repeatedly over a period of time. In standard English *he is working* can be used for cases both of immediacy and of duration. If the Negro nonstandard English speaker is instructed to use *he is working* without explicitly discussing the different uses in standard English and Negro nonstandard English, he may use *he is working* for immediate situations only (therefore really not speaking standard English though using standard English forms) and may hypercorrect *he be working* to *he bees working* to denote a kind of duration.

Unfortunately the Center for Applied Linguistics' materials, although based on a more sophisticated understanding of language and a quite thorough knowledge of both standard English and Negro nonstandard English (like many of the "second-language learning" programs for Negro inner-city children), have not been evaluated in a teaching context. However, the Center materials have the distinct advantage of having been developed in the field situation and used in the classroom, and thus the course developers were able to get initial impressions concerning the efficiency and effectiveness of their lessons.

If we presume that materials to teach standard English as a second dialect can be developed and that specialists can be trained to teach with them and to generate more material, the question still remains how shall such a specialist be incorporated into the school system. It seems that the answer to such a question depends upon the level at which the new material is introduced.

Teaching the details of standard English in junior high and high school might well be treated as a separate course. Kenneth Johnson has indicated that teaching standard English as a separate subject as opposed to incorporating it within the existing language arts curriculum may well be the most effective approach.[22] Giving the specialist the role of standard English teacher with emphasis on oral language proficiency clearly denotes a function in the same way that the French teacher's role is identifiable. In the same way that the

---

22K. Johnson, "An Evaluation of Second Language Techniques for Teaching Standard English to Negro Students," *NCTE* paper, 1968.

French teacher must be trained in second-language techniques, French language, French culture and history, the standard English teacher must be trained in second-language techniques, Negro nonstandard English, and Afro-American culture and history. The standard English teacher, unlike the English teacher who wishes to teach the formal aspects of a language as well as stylistic conventions—i.e., the business letter, the essay, etc.—to students who already know the language, understands her job as teaching standard English to nonstandard English speakers. She does not assume they know the language she is teaching.

3. *The role of the specialist.* What the role of the specialist in the preschool and elementary school should be is less clear. If we had a distinct bilingual situation here, one might suggest that the specialist actually teach the primary grades in Negro nonstandard English while incorporating procedures for teaching standard English into the curriculum. However, one of the distinctions between a school which must deal with children who speak a different language as opposed to a school where a different dialect is taught involves mutual intelligibility. A class full of non-English speaking children with a teacher who speaks only English will no doubt have to resort to gestures and pictures in order to function at all. This is not true in the case of Negro nonstandard-English-speaking children and a standard-English-speaking teacher. With a little bit of tuning in on both the teacher and the children's part and with a shared vocabulary the classroom is able to "function" from the very beginning although they speak differently. However, continued failure of many black inner-city schools indicates that this kind of functioning is not adequate.

The most effective use of the specialist at the primary level might be as classroom teacher. In this role she could use her knowledge of Negro nonstandard English to teach the child standard English and to aid the child in his initial attempts to read.[23] Although she would use standard English as the medium of instruction (except when she is contrasting standard English and Negro nonstandard English) she would allow the children to use Negro nonstandard English in responding (except of course when she was teaching standard

---

[23]The Education Study Center is currently involved in a reading project in the District of Columbia using dialect texts as initial readers.

English) thereby not confusing knowledge of standard English with knowledge of the subject matter — science, math, etc. — to be learned.[24] As the child progressed through the primary grades and became more proficient in standard English, use of more standard English could be demanded within the classroom. Such an approach would allow the child to learn the expected language response system before he was required to use it. Of course, a program such as the one discussed above is proposed on the assumption that it is both possible and efficient to teach young children standard English using a "quasi-foreign language" approach. This assumption should be tested.

Conclusion

This paper has attempted to deal with some of the issues involved in educating black children who do not speak standard English. Questions have been raised whether these children should learn standard English, who should teach them, how a specialist should be trained, and what such specialists should do. This author firmly believes that the success of black children in our public school system is very much dependent upon the teacher's recognition of the fact that these children may not speak standard English, and that if they do not speak standard English, formal instruction in the language arts cannot continue to be predicated on the assumption that all the children know standard English. The dialect of black nonstandard speaking children must be incorporated into the curriculum as part of the process of teaching these children standard English skills. Only then can such a child learn a second dialect (standard English) without experiencing shame and humiliation towards his native dialect.

---

[24] I remember being in a third grade class that was discussing the Revolutionary War. The teacher asked "Who crossed the Delaware River with troops? A young Negro boy responded "Dat George Washington" to which the teacher replied "No, that was George Washington." With such a correction the class, I am sure, was confused as to the right answer and the boy learned not to volunteer information again!

12. Barriers to Successful Reading for Second-Language Students at the Secondary Level

Joyce Morris

Because the children of linguistic minorities often do not speak English when they come to school, they have more trouble than others in learning to read English. The first place they are noticed by the school is often in the remedial reading class, whether at primary school or secondary school. Many of these "backward readers" turn out to be speakers of another language whose special problem has so far been ignored. The question is presented by Joyce Morris in a paper that was originally given at the 1968 TESOL Convention. Professor Morris now teaches in the Department of Elementary Education of San Diego State College. For further detail on the topic, a good collection is *Reading for the Disadvantaged: Problems of Linguistically Different Learners*, edited by Thomas D. Horn (New York: Harcourt, Brace and World, Inc., 1970).

In several years of visiting reading classes in New Mexico, I have had the opportunity to observe the reading of Indian and Spanish-American children who were non-English speakers. Two examples may serve to illustrate the nature of some of their reading difficulties: 1) An eighth grade Navajo girl read a poem containing the line "He married his girl with a golden band . . . " The girl read the line perfectly in that she pronounced all the words correctly. However, when asked what was meant by this line, she was unable to explain it. 2) A Spanish-speaking boy was asked the meaning of the word *brave.* He replied that when something was put over your face, you couldn't "brave" (breathe). Aside from specific examples of reading-language confusion, I have been struck by the fact that we

Reprinted from the TESOL Quarterly, 2 (1968), pages 158-63, by permission of the author and the publishers.

accept, as perfectly normal, the fact that we have entire classrooms of Indian students at the junior high school level who are reading at the second or third grade level. These children are graduated from high school with, perhaps, intermediate grade level reading ability. Several years ago I tutored Indian students at the University of New Mexico. The majority of these students were performing at approximately a fourth or fifth grade reading level as measured by a standardized test.[1] When we consider the fact that standardized tests generally overestimate true reading ability, the degree of reading retardation becomes even greater.

This situation is not new, nor is the fact that these problems become even more pronounced the longer the child stays in school. Let's take a brief look at what we know of the achievement of the non-English-speaking children in our schools.

1. In 1936, Loyd Tireman found that Spanish-speaking children in Albuquerque became more academically retarded the higher they advanced through the grades:[2]

Fourth Grade   .... 7 months retardation
Fifth Grade   ..... 1.1 years retardation
Sixth Grade   ..... 1.8 years retardation
Seventh Grade   ... 2.3 years retardation

2. In 1958, in studying the achievement of Indian children for the Bureau of Indian Affairs, Madison Coombs documented the same trend toward progressive retardation.[3]

3. In 1960, Boyce found that Indian children were achieving at grade level at the end of the second grade, but that by the end of the sixth grade they were two or more years retarded.[4]

4. In 1961, Townsend tested 558 eleventh and twelfth grade Indian students in selected high schools in Albuquerque. He found

[1] Miles V. Zintz and Joyce Morris, *Tutoring-Counseling Program for Indian Students, 1960-62* (Albuquerque: University of New Mexico, College of Education, 1962).

[2] Loyd S. Tireman, *Teaching Spanish-Speaking Children* (Albuquerque: The University of New Mexico Press, 1948), p. 68.

[3] L. Madison Coombs, et al., "The Indian Child goes to School" (Washington, D.C.: U.S. Department of Interior, Bureau of Indian Affairs, 1958), p. 3.

[4] George Boyce, "Why Do Indians Quit School?" *Indian Education,* No. 344 (Lawrence, Kansas: Haskell Institute, May, 1960, p. 5.

that 73 percent of the eleventh graders, and 65 percent of the twelfth graders were achieving at a level below the 20th percentile rank. Further analysis showed that 54 percent of the eleventh graders and 51 percent of the twelfth graders fell below the 10th percentile rank in reading achievement.[5]

5. In 1964, Smith surveyed the achievement of Indian children in New Mexico schools, and found the following to be characteristic in terms on age in grade:[6]

Grade	Of Age In Grade	1 Year Retarded In Grade	2 Years Retarded In Grade	3 or More Years Retarded In Grade
1	40%	43%	12%	5%
6	28%	38%	22%	14%
9	28%	46%	21%	7%
12	25%	42%	23%	11%

6. In 1966, the Coleman Report found that all minority groups (excluding Orientals) score distinctly lower than the children of the dominant group, and the degree of the discrepancy in achievement is greatest in the twelfth grade, a finding that led Bruce Gaarder of the U. S. Office of Education to remark that " . . . Indian children lose ground the longer they stay in school."[7]

Now that we have established the fact that these children are able to achieve at grade level through the primary grades but that their level of achievement from that point on is an endless downward spiral, let's look at some of the possible reasons for this.

In the primary grades there is high interest in the initial decoding process. Children have a real sense of accomplishment in learning to say what is written on the page. This is the acquisition of a new and

[5]Irving D. Townsend, "The Reading Achievement of Eleventh and Twelfth Grade Indian Students and a Survey of Curricular Changes Indicated for the Improved Teaching of Reading in the Public High Schools of New Mexico," Diss., The University of New Mexico (1961), p. 118.

[6]Anne M. Smith, *New Mexico Indians Today: A Report Prepared as Part of the New Mexico State Resources Development Plan* (Santa Fe, 1965), p. 47.

[7]Bruce Gaarder, "Education of American Indian Children," in *Reports of the Annual Conference of the Southwest Council of Foreign Language Teachers at El Paso, Texas* (November, 1967), p. 33.

highly valued skill, and motivation is not the problem it becomes at higher grade levels. In addition, the vocabulary and the concepts the small child is asked to master both are rigidly controlled and are within the grasp of the learner. The primary school teacher is with the child all day, all year, and becomes intimately acquainted with him and with his specific needs and weaknesses. She can make time throughout the day to provide special help. Perhaps most important, in these years school is important to the child. He has fewer outside interests, and his teacher and his school work loom large in his life.

In the intermediate grades, there is a sudden and tremendous increase in the difficulty of vocabulary, content, and concepts that the child is expected to cope with. There is more pressure for academic achievement, and more emphasis on speed. The carefully controlled content and vocabulary of earlier grades breaks down here, and children are expected to learn, at a faster rate, more complex material in various content areas.

This same trend continues into the junior high years, and it is in these years that many teachers feel that now the children have learned to read and that from here on they simply read to learn. Just at the point where materials become more complex, as the quantity of reading increases, and as more refined reading skills are demanded—only too often—instruction in reading stops.

At the high school level there is even more content to master in less time; the teacher's time with each child is far less; and if the child has been having trouble with reading, the years of frustration and failure have killed his interest in learning to read *or* in reading to learn.

It may fairly be said that the above description fits many children and is not true only of the English-as-a-second-language learner. When speaking of this child, we realize that there are additional barriers to reading success. Obviously, the major problem of these children is the fact that they have little or no facility with the English language. This is so obvious that it has often been said that teaching reading to these children is, in reality, teaching English as a second language. It certainly can't be denied that in initial reading instruction command of the oral language must precede reading, and that in teaching reading we must observe the principles of TESOL: hearing, speaking, reading, writing. A few remarks of adult Indians illustrate their recognition of the importance of learning English:

If you could learn English, the other things related, it would come and open your mind, because you could begin to read, and pick up a book and read and understand—Here's a good occupation I could be training for. But with a minimum of English and no true challenge, well, the Indian is bound to take the lazy way out.

I think if they want us to speak English, if they want us to have a really good command of English and thereby as a result get along in the world of the white man, I think English should be emphasized at the beginning stages . . . We don't have good enough command of English to communicate effectively.

I didn't really learn English, though a graduate of BIA boarding school, until I went to Bacone and I began to feel that I could understand the newspaper, and really pick up a book and read it for pleasure or understanding, and I was no longer *simulating* understanding. Before Bacone I did recognize a few words and this and that but my vocabulary was very poor.[8]

Contributions from linguists have impressed on us that learning a language is not just learning words, but that pitch, structure, intonation, and the cultural setting are all a part of language learning. Further, the recognition of the importance of first teaching regular pronunciation and spelling patterns in beginning reading has influenced classroom practices. The value for the children in paying careful attention to phoneme-grapheme correspondence in beginning reading instruction has led to the development of improved beginning reading programs.

However, there are a few points that disturb me when we talk of applying TESOL approaches to secondary reading instruction. First of all, we know that lack of facility with English handicaps the child in learning to read English, *but,* conversely, we cannot say that the ability to speak English will insure ability to read English. If this were true, we would not have estimates from 10 percent to 15 percent of the general school population struggling with reading retardation. We know that it is possible for the upper-class Anglo child who has an above average command of the oral language to have serious reading problems at the high school and college levels.

---

[8] Smith, p. 54.

My second point is that teaching oral English and teaching reading are not identical processes and do not have the same purposes. In the first we are concerned with oral production, and here the aural-oral techniques are effective. In teaching reading, we do not want the student to pronounce each word. A truly efficient reader uses a minimum of oral production, or even "mental pronunciation," as he reads.

The third point is that the processes and aims of initial reading instruction and advanced reading instruction are by no means the same. In initial reading instruction, the learner is learning how to break the code. He is learning that the symbols (graphemes) represent sounds—that writing is indeed "talk written down." In the first grade, perceptual skills and visual and auditory discrimination are necessary for success. However, at higher levels the ability to form and use concepts increases in importance. One study shows that by the fifth grade concept formation is more closely related to reading achievement than is IQ.[9]

Studies of concept formation and learning have shown us: (1) that concept development is facilitated when the child (or adult) has had concrete experiences on which to base his concepts; (2) that the wider variety of associations the child can make with the concept, the easier it is to learn and to retain; (3) that the more *meaningful* the ideas to be assimilated, the easier the learning and retention; and (4) that a concept, once formed, is represented by a symbol, and that the symbol is usually a word. The word then becomes sufficient in itself to trigger the release of the meanings of the concepts it represents.

Think of frequently used words, such as *democracy, hatred, patriotism,* or *prejudice,* and I think we will all realize that what comes to mind is not a dictionary definition, but a flood of feelings, emotions, and opinions that have been formed by innumerable past experiences, both real and vicarious.

In short, at higher levels we do not want children to equate words with sounds but with *meanings.* We do not want them to translate from graphemes to phonemes—we want them to be unaware of graphemes, as most of us are, and to grasp from the printed page the

[9]Jean Braun, "Relationship Between Concept Formation and Reading Achievement," *Child Development,* 34 (September, 1963), 675-82.

concepts, feelings, and opinions put there by the writer. The purpose of reading at the secondary level is usually not to teach the students to decode the written symbols—that is, to produce the corresponding speech forms—but to explore, interpret, and extend the concepts represented by the written symbols. The major weakness in the reading of ESL students at the secondary level is the fact that, in all too many instances, the initial reading step is performed: the child decodes the symbols and produces the word—and stops. The word fails to trigger *anything* because the concepts it represents to us and to the author simply do not exist for the child, or they exist in a limited, vague form.

This is the point where, in my opinion, our teaching of English and reading breaks down. We must realize that reading is a skill and a tool, and as such is meant to be used to extend knowledge. Teaching children to pronounce words, and *assuming* that they have meaning for the child is not teaching reading. Too many of us are guilty of limiting the children's ideas of what reading is by our acceptance of word calling without real understanding. We spend a great deal of time on workbook exercises calling for filling in blanks with words that can be found by a process of elimination. Questions teachers ask are usually concerned with simple repetition of fact and do not lead the children to develop or extend reading. Guzsak found that over 70 percent of teacher questions at the elementary level asked for simple recall.[10]

In addition to teaching children to pronounce words, we must also provide experiences—whether these experiences be real or vicarious—that will make the words mean something once they have been decoded. Certainly we cannot bring war, germs, or the Detroit riots into the classroom so that concepts may be formed through concrete experiences, but we can use audio-visual aids, field trips, or conversations with those who have had real experience with such things.

In addition we must enlist—or demand—the help of all teachers in developing meaning. Those in other content areas are best equipped to teach the concepts and the vocabulary of their particular

---

[10]Frank Guzsak, "Teacher Questioning and Reading," *The Reading Teacher,* 21: 3 (December, 1967), 227-234.

field, and they must do this. The English and reading teacher cannot bear the entire burden.

Test results, teacher comments, and personal experience and observation support the major assumption I have made here: that *meaning,* and not oral production, is the greatest problem encountered in the teaching of both English and reading to the secondary school student of ESL. Reading test scores of Indian students reveal that they consistently score lower in comprehension than in the mechanics of reading. Comments of teachers of Indian children are equally consistent: "They're word callers, but they don't have any idea what the words mean." Those dealing with Navajo children have one universal remark to make: "They just can't deal with abstractions. Everything must be concrete; and even then, only the literal interpretation is made." Perhaps this is interference of the native language and thought patterns, but we must also consider that maybe they have never had the opportunity to develop the conceptual basis for abstraction in English.

Most of our knowledge is gained through reading. Without reading skill the best and most profitable path to knowledge is blocked, as is the path to what we call "the mainstream of American life." By accepting a limited version of reading we are limiting the child's educational career and his later life. We are actually advocating a different kind of reading for the non-English speaker from that we consider suitable for the Anglo child. We have had a great deal of help from linguists in terms of increasing our knowledge of what our language is really like, and we have had help from the foreign-language teachers regarding methods and techniques of second-language teaching. But now we need to move on and ask how—once the children have mastered the initial oral language and reading skills—we can proceed to the development of real thinking and concept formation ability in the new language. We cannot be satisfied with less.

13. The Language of Tests for Young Children

Graeme Kennedy

To find out something about its pupils and their progress, schools use tests. Standardized tests are widely used in the belief that they are a fair and reliable method of recognizing educational achievement. But most standardized tests are written in English and have been standardized with native speakers of English. This means that children whose native language is not English are often classified as being educationally retarded or of low intelligence. In the following paper, which reports research carried out at UCLA under a contract with the U.S. Office of Education, Dr. Graeme Kennedy, now a lecturer in English at Victoria University of Wellington, analyzes in some detail the way that tests are often unsuitable for young children and for nonnative speakers of English.

OVERVIEW

It is very likely that many young children attempting to take aptitude and achievement tests do not correctly comprehend the general instructions, let alone some of the individual test items. For example, children of grades one and two, attempting the California Achievement Test, received the instruction — *Do not turn this page until told to do so.* While this is a simple, straightforward instruction for an adult, it can be incomprehensible for a child of six years, because this sentence, unnecessarily, includes at least three linguistic devices which recent studies of comprehension have shown to be difficult for young children. First, *deletions* have been shown to

Originally published as Working Paper No. 7, Center for the Study of Education, Graduate School of Education, University of California, Los Angeles, and reprinted by permission of the author.

affect children's comprehension adversely. Thus, *until told to do so* would almost certainly be easier in the undeleted form – *until you are told to do so.* Second, numerous researchers have shown that sentences in the passive voice are much harder for children to understand than sentences in the active voice. Thus, *until (you are) told to do so* would undoubtedly be easier in the form – *until I tell you to do it.* Finally, the presence of both a negative *and* the temporal conjunction *until* in the sentence would cause some children to hesitate in comprehending the sentence or to misinterpret it altogether. Thus, *Do not turn this page until . . .* would almost certainly be easier in the form *Turn this page (only) when . . .*

This paper will outline some of the ways in which the language of the test instrument can be a factor in affecting the performance of a given child or group of children on a test. Though format, cognitive complexity of a task, memory load, and conceptual demands also affect comprehension, these nonlinguistic factors will not be discussed here.

In most tests, language is treated as if it were a neutral vehicle by means of which task requirements are communicated to the person being tested. This person, in return, reveals his cognitive skills, knowledge, aptitudes, and/or achievement with specific verbal or nonverbal behaviors. Although language is never really a neutral vehicle, language difficulties for certain types of tests are probably not very great in that the task requirements do not involve complex instructions for each item. For example, in the Illinois Test of Psycholinguistic Abilities there is good reason to assume that language is a relatively neutral factor in affecting test performance. In this test, certain psycholinguistic abilities rather than specific achievements are being assessed and there is a minimum of linguistic complexity and variation in the task instructions. Similarly, in certain tests of verbal intelligence, in which the factors constituting verbal intelligence are not clearly understood, the test instrument as a whole, including both task requirements and the language used to convey these requirements, may be a self-authenticating instrument with prognostic value.

However, in tests of quantitative intelligence, mathematical skills, conceptual knowledge, readiness, and aptitude, it is not reasonable to think of the language of the test as a neutral factor. It is with such tests that this paper is especially concerned.

In the typical test situation with children, there are three major language users involved.

1. The test designer (an educated adult)
2. The child
3. The tester (presumably an educated adult)

To the extent that the *language* of the test does not match the language development and the dialect of the child, and to the extent that the speech of the tester does not match the speech with which the child is familiar, the child's test performance will be influenced adversely.

THE LANGUAGE OF THE TEST
AND THE LANGUAGE OF THE CHILD

These may differ on both developmental and subcultural grounds, and will be discussed separately.

Developmental Differences

Developmental differences between adult and child language affecting *comprehension* are probably much greater than has generally been recognized. Until recently, views like those of Carroll (1960) were widely accepted. "After the age of six, there is relatively little in the grammar or syntax of the language that the average child needs to learn." However, recent studies of the comprehension of syntax by children from the age of about two to ten, in reasonably simple areas of syntax, have indicated that it is not reasonable to assume that children understand syntax at the same level as adults and certainly not reasonable to conclude that the child *knows* his language by the time he begins school. Moreover, Carol Chomsky (1968) has noted that even in certain trivial areas of English syntax, there is evidence of highly individual rates of development in comprehension ability.

Very few areas of English grammar have been studied from the point of view of development of comprehension, but those areas which have been studied tend to show that basic linguistic processes are still being mastered at the second-grade level, and that some processes are not fully acquired until age eleven or twelve. For example, Slobin (1966) in a study with children from six to twelve, showed that passive sentences took significantly longer to respond to than semantically equivalent active sentences. That is, *The dog was being chased by the cat* took longer than *The cat was chasing the dog* at all age levels. That this result could not be attributed entirely to differences in sentence length is indicated by other studies which show that passive sentences are both intrinsically harder and later in development than active sentences. For example, Beilin and Spontak (1969) report that at first-grade level, a test of comprehension of active and passive sentences showed 93 percent correct responses to active sentences and 73 percent to equivalent passive sentences. The students were required to select one picture from two presented to them to match a sentence they heard. The sentences were very simple, e.g., *Mark hits Susan; Susan is hit by Mark.* When the sentences were made complex with an indirect object e.g., *John gave Mary a book; Mary was given a book by John,* correct comprehension of the passive deteriorated markedly. Whereas 93 percent of the responses to active sentences continued to be correct, only 23 percent of the responses to passives were correct.

Test writers assume 100 percent comprehenison of the language of the test, and yet test instructions, test items, and task requirements are typically much more complex than those in the experiment by Beilin and Spontak, where much less than 100 percent comprehension was achieved by six-year-olds.

Another syntactic area studied in recent years is conjunction. Hatch (1969) found that with sentences containing such temporal conjunctions as *before, when, after,* where the order of clauses can be juxtaposed, children up to the age of at least seven respond more correctly and more rapidly when the order of action stated in a sentence is the same as the order of the action required. For example, a child finds it much easier to understand (a) than (b).

(a) *Move a blue piece before you move a red piece.*
(b) *Before you move a red piece, move a blue piece.*
(a) *After you move a blue piece move a red piece.*
(b) *Move a red piece after you move a blue piece.*

Similarly, on a relatively simple task testing comprehension of conditional sentences using *unless,* second graders consistently continue to interpret *unless* as *if* rather than as *if not;* i.e., *Unless you are quiet, we won't go* is interpreted as meaning the same as *If you are quiet, we won't go.* Five-year olds correctly comprehended only about 50 percent of sentences containing *if*. A study by Olds (1968) indicates that difficulty with sentences containing clauses beginning with *unless* continues to at least nine years of age. The Olds and Hatch studies together suggest that while conditional sentences seem to be consistently misunderstood by five-year-olds, some children will have difficulty understanding them as late as nine years of age. (It is worth noting that Olds's subjects were upper middle-class boys.)

Both these studies were particularly concerned with comprehension of *if* and *unless*. The most difficult part of comprehending conditional sentences, however, is not associated with *if* and *unless*. Rather, learning to comprehend some of the at least 324 possible verb-form combinations, which in turn can interact with negation in one, or both clauses, poses a major difficulty for comprehension. A comparative study of this problem has not yet been undertaken.

However, tests given to children frequently contain conditional sentences. A case in point is the *California Achievement Tests* (lower primary, grades one and two). In the General Instructions and before each subtest the children are told - *If you do not know an answer, go on to the next question.* It seems possible that some children of that age will transpose the *not* to the second clause in interpreting the sentence as *do not go to the next question.* In the same instructions, the children are told, *You may do very well even if you do not finish everything.* Again, it seems likely that some children, weak in comprehending sentences containing *if,* will merely respond to the last part of the sentence – *do not finish everything.*

The form of questions or instructions employed in a test is another syntactic area which may seriously affect comprehension. There is a basic grammatical distinction between questions permitting a *Yes/No* answer and those which do not, e.g.,

1. *Is the red one bigger than the green one? (Yes/No)*
2. *Which one is bigger?*

For sentence two, a *Yes/No* answer is not possible and such questions are almost certainly more difficult than type one sentences. However, there are also degrees of difficulty for type two questions and instructions, although very little is known about this.

(cf., Fodor, 1969; Hatch et al., 1969). Children respond differently to instructions like:

1. *What did X do?*
(one is easier than two)
2. *Tell me about X.*

They find sentence one easier than sentence two. Similarly, children take a good deal less time to respond to sentence four than to sentence three, even though four is longer. (Fodor, 1969).

3. *Ask him the time.*
4. *Ask him what the time is.*

The growing literature on the comprehension of English comparatives (bigger, more, less, etc.,) and on *conservation* suggests that poor comprehension of linguistic devices may be the cause of the failure of many children on a *conservation task.* For example, Donaldson and Balfour (1968) showed that as late as 4.7 years children interpreted *less* as meaning *more* with discrete objects, in a variety of task situations. Rothenberg (1969) indicates that only 78 percent of children of 4.3 to 6.0 years from middle-class homes can consistently respond correctly both to sentences with *more* and sentences with *same,* while another 10 percent comprehended *same* correctly but not *more.* With black children from lower-class homes only 30 percent comprehended both, and an additional *52 percent* could comprehend *same* but not *more.* Rothenberg's conclusion was that even in this apparently simple and straightforward area of comparison, different children will not respond identically to different ways of saying the same thing. Thus, while one child will understand a task requirement if the instruction is given in one form, another child will not. Kennedy (1970), in a study with children ages six to ten, found that the various linguistic devices used to make comparisons are hierarchically ordered in difficulty according to whether the comparison is made in terms of equality (easiest), superiority, or inferiority (hardest). In a comparision task it seems clear that it may be necessary to ask a question in two or more different ways in order to make the task requirement clear to all children.

1. *Does X have more than Y?*
2. *Does Y have less than X?*

3. *Does X have as many as Y? etc.*

It should be noted that Labov *et al.* (1968), in their study of Black Urban Dialect of New York City, point out that problems with comparatives are among the most difficult for speakers of both standard and nonstandard English.

So far, possible difficulties in comprehension based on a very small number of rather simple syntactic factors have been mentioned. It is obvious that individual words will also often cause failure of comprehension of test items for individual subjects. Thus, a child being tested for aptitude with spatial relationships can hardly be faulted on his "knowledge" if he reacts in bewilderment when he is told to *"Put the dodecahedron halfway along the bottom line."* Most test writers have recognized this problem and have carefully selected commonly known lexical items in tasks for children. They have not always been careful enough, however, as the following example from the California Achievement Tests for grades one to two indicates; *This game will show how well you can recognize words with opposite meanings.* It is possible that six-year-olds will not understand *recognize* and that they will struggle with *opposite meanings.* It is especially noteworthy that *opposite* is used in Section C of the test as *opposite meanings* (i.e., semantically antonymous) whereas in Section D the children are told that there are some words *opposite* a picture (i.e., spatially adjacent). It would not be surprising if some six-year-olds were confused or hesitant when faced with such instructions.

There is another important way in which the particular lexical items used in a test may affect comprehension and result in false interpretations of the test performance being made. At the present time there is a growing interest in tests of conceptual aptitude, and here especially language can be a confounding factor, because failure of comprehension of language is frequently interpreted as cognitive deficiency.

There are indications that test writers do not always recognize that a test of a child's mastery of concepts may in fact test only the child's comprehension of verbal labels, and that there is an important distinction between concepts and verbal labels (cf. Carroll, 1964). Concepts are cognitive classifying constructs formed on the basis of perceptual experience. One learns to classify experience and to label these *classifications*, not the direct references.

This can be illustrated by considering the comprehension of the quantitative concept which in English is labeled *enough*. The word *enough* labels a concept which people form from experiencing a large number of positive and negative instances of *enoughness*. No single physical example or simple verbal definition can convey the psychological complexities involved in comprehending the concept, which may be labeled with words and phrases like *enough, adequate, sufficient, just right, not too much, the right amount, we don't need any more,* and so on.

It is important to make the distinction between concepts and the linguistic devices which express them, because, while not knowing labels is undoubtedly a problem for school learning, it does not necessarily imply cognitive deficiency. Presumably a monolingual French child of normal intelligence would fail a test of *concepts* administered to him in English. When a child, after living for six years in the typically human environment of color, numerical equality and inequality, time, space, etc., performs poorly on a test of certain *critical* concepts of color, number, and so on, it is often implied that there is something inadequate in the child's cognitive capacity and functioning and many conclude that such children are *deficient* in their conceptual behavior. It rarely seems to occur to those who jump to such conclusions that the children's poor performance might be due to the language of the test which proved difficult to process. When a child is given a test item (e. g. —*Mark the cup which has sufficient water for a drink*) and makes an inappropriate response, it cannot be legitimately concluded that the child has not learned the concept of *enoughness*. Thus, a test which ostensibly tests for knowledge of concepts, but which in fact tests for comprehension of verbal labels, can lead to false interpretations of the nature of the child's performance problems, interpretations which are of educational and personal significance.

A recent test which illustrates this confounding of concepts and labels and a number of other language difficulties is that by Boehm (1969). "Before he can read . . . does he understand what others are telling him?" challenges an introduction describing the test. The test is designed "to measure children's mastery of concepts . . . . It may be used to identify *children* with deficiences .... and to identify individual *concepts* on which children could profit from instruction .... As many as 60 out of 100 children entering kindergarten may be unable to mark the *right end* of a line or to indicate the area *below* a pictured table." Moreover, children from different backgrounds start out "with a different body of knowledge and set of understandings." Such differences are called "variations in cognitive development."

A close examination of the test, however, shows that these apparently lofty goals—assessing differences in cognitive development—are hopelessly confused with comprehension of English. This can be seen in a number of places in the test. For example, there is syntactic ambiguity in Question 1. The children are asked to *mark the paper with the star at the top.* (The concept being tested is top). This sentence is potentially ambiguous.

(a) *Mark the paper which has a star at the top.* (Intended)
(b) *Mark a star at the top of the paper.*

In Question 15 there is possible confusion based on phonology. *Mark the cake that is whole (whole* is the concept being tested). The children are presented with these pictures.

It is very likely that some children will hear *Mark the cake that has (a) hole.*

In Question 24 there is possible confusion based on lexical misunderstanding. The children are asked to *Look at the bottles. Mark the one that is almost empty* (knowledge of *almost* is being tested. There are pictures of three bottles presented—one almost full, one half full, one almost empty.) However, if a child who understands *almost* does not understand *empty* which is *not* being tested he could very easily make the wrong selection.

In Question 28 there is possible confusion based on mishearing function words.
Mark the circle that is at a side of the box could be heard *as Mark the circle that is outside of the box.*

In Question 29 there is confusion of parts of speech on the part of the test writer. Ostensibly this question tests knowledge of the concept *beginning.* It is not stated, but it is to be assumed, that the question intended to test *beginning* as a noun. Yet in the test sentence, the child is asked to *Mark the squirrel that is beginning to climb the tree. Beginning* is the present participle of the *verb* and it may be asked why this particular form of the verb was tested and not the more frequent forms of *begin, began, will begin.*

In Question 33, the plausibility of the question and required answer are problems. This is supposed to be a test of *never. Look at the chair, the apple, and the cookies. Mark what a child should never eat.* It is quite conceivable that a child would consider he should never eat the leaf and stalk of the apple in the picture, or never eat cookies because they are bad for his teeth.

Question 36 is a test of *always.* (The child sees a picture of a dog, a book, and an ear.) Whereas in Question 33, a test of *never,* the child was asked *Mark what a child should never eat,* in Question 36 he is asked to *Mark the one a child always has.* For very similar kinds of tasks the syntax of the test question is obviously different. There are indications that Question 33 is syntactically much easier than Question 36.

Apart from such linguistic factors as these, potentially interfering with particular children's comprehension of what they are required to do, the real confusion of concepts and labels is seen in a comparison of Questions 7 and 32. In 7 the children have to mark on a row of five flowers the *one in the middle.* In 32, they have to mark on a line of three cars, *the one that is not the first nor the last.* Clearly the same concept is being tested in both questions.

Thus, what is essentially a simple vocabulary test is dressed up as a test of cognitive development, the results of which can be highly misleading and could lead to labeling children as having inadequacies in their intellectual processes.

Other possible bases of difficulties about which almost nothing is known, but about which nothing should be assumed, include the effect of sentence length on comprehension and the effect of ambiguity. Menyuk (1969) indicates that with children from three to six years, in sentences of up to nine words, the length of the sentence is not a critical factor in comprehension. Rather the internal structure of the sentence seems to be the critical variable. However, *very* long sentences, well above nine words, are not uncommon in tests; e.g., *You are to count the number of things in each box in the first row and then draw a line to the box in the second row that shows this number (30 words). Study the minute hand and the hour hand of each clock. Then write the number that tells the correct time for each clock in the space in the sentence below it (20 words).*

These sentences, found in the *California Achievement Tests* for grades one and two, place severe strains on the short-term memory capacity of all children of that age. By losing track of the task requirement, faulty comprehension and a misleading test performance will certainly result. Apart from the length and complexity of the instructions in the above examples, it may very well be true that six-year-olds do not know what a *sentence* is, what the *correct* time is, or even what it means to *study* a minute hand.

The effect of ambiguity, and the child's ability to detect ambiguity, is a matter about which practically nothing is known. Transformational grammarians have pointed out that the ability to disambiguate sentences and to recognize ambiguity is an indication of a person's competence—his knowledge of the rules of the grammar of his language. Further, this ability is used as partial evidence for the kind of grammatical model used by transformational grammarians. What is not know is whether what is ambiguous for adults is unambiguous for children and vice versa. That there may well be important differences is suggested by differences in the structure of associations. It has been established, for example, by Brown and Berko (1960), Ervin-Tripp (1961), Entwisle *et al.* (1964), that until about seven years, children tend to give syntagmatic associations to stimulus words, whereas older children and adults give paradigmatic associations. That is, when presented with the stimulus word *black,* young children tend to give an association like *cat* or *book,* belonging to a different grammatical class, whereas adults give a word in the same part of speech—e.g., *white* or *red.* It is very likely that words which are unambiguous for adults are not so for children, whose lexical and semantic systems are much less developed. As a case in point, the Cattell (1950) *Culture Fair Test* for children aged four to eight years, contains the following ambiguous sentence: *I want you to put the same marks under the same pictures below the line.* An adult will presumably make the *commonsense* reaction and interpret *same* as meaning *similar* and make marks beneath other pictures which are below the line. If a child interprets *same* as meaning *exactly identical,* (cf., Braine and Shanks, 1965) he may interpret *below the line* as referring not to *the same (similar) pictures (which are) below the line* but rather as the place under the original pictures where he is to make his mark.

Subcultural Differences

In the previous section, it was noted that poor comprehension could result from particular labels for concepts not being known by certain children. Across subcultures and dialectal differences such as those found between Standard American English and the Black Urban Dialect, such difference in verbal labels can be even greater. However, there are other basic problems resulting from subcultural differences and some of these will be discussed.

While the differences between adult and child language constitute a kind of dialectal or subcultural difference (e.g., in the child's use of telegraphese), a much greater dialectal difference affecting test performance can be seen in the effect of socioeconomic status and subcultural group membership. That subcultural differences are important has long been recognized by, for example, attempts to prepare *culture-free* tests. However, the well known *IPAT Culture Fair Test* by Cattell (1950) is phrased in terms of Standard American English and thus cannot be considered unbiased or culture-fair for speakers of other dialects. In fact, the prose style of the test is strangely awkward even within the standard dialect. Consider, for example, the following sentence from oral instructions for Test One for children four to eight years of age. *Now finish the row and go on with the other rows to the bottom of the page, putting always under each picture the mark that belongs under it.* Even if the last part of this sentence is accepted as being grammatically correct, it is nevertheless tortured prose style.

The importance of the test administrator belonging to the same ethnic group as the child being tested has been emphasized by some. However, the importance of language dialect differences on test performance is apparently severely underestimated. In order that a child understand task requirements it is not enough that the test administrator be of the same race and speak clearly. It is important too that he or she speak the same dialect. In addition to the developmental differences between the language of the child and the language of the test, outlined above, if the dialect of the child is different from the standard dialect in which the test is written, the test could be considerably more difficult for him. For example, in the following sentences the same information is communicated in two different dialects, one General Standard American (G.S.A.), the other, the Black Urban Dialect of New York City as described by Labov *et al.*, 1968. It should be emphasized that these differences are *syntactic* and are in addition to the phonological differences between the two dialects.

G.S.A.: *He's always doing that (He does that all the time).*
B.U.D.: *He be doin' that all the time.*
G.S.A.: *It isn't always her fault.*
B.U.D.: *It don't be always her fault.*
G.S.A.: *He's taller than you.*
B.U.D.: *He's more taller than you.*
G.S.A.: *He can run as fast as I can.*
B.U.D.: *He can run the same fas' as I can.*
G.S.A.: *She has the same accent as her mother.*
B.U.D.: *She got the same accent of her mother.*
G.S.A.: *I know he won the most awards in track.*
B.U.D.: *I know he was the most award winner in track.*
G.S.A.: *When you watch a game, you don't get as much fun as you would if you were actually playing it.*
B.U.D.: *When you watchin' a game, you ain't gitting that much fun than what you would really be playing it.*

These differences may seem to be trivial but are not, since they are syntactic and thus involve the basic structure of the language. What seems probable, furthermore, is that the cumulation of differences, however slight, in sentence after sentence can increase processing time for a person who is not a native speaker of that dialect, and if the differences are too great, can create inaccurate processing, if not complete lack of comprehension.

The examples given above are mostly of simple short sentences, and the difficulties for a child of six years speaking one of the dialects and being tested in the other, can only be guessed at. As was noted, the differences above are syntactic. Across subcultures there are typically different distributions of the lexicon as well which will compound the difficulties. It is hypothesized that this effect can be expected to occur for urban black children being tested in the standard dialect or for white children being tested in the black urban dialect.

The Speech of the Test Administrator

In any test in which the instructions and/or the specific test items are orally administered, the speech of the examiner can have an important influence on comprehension. In addition to obvious dialect differences between the adult and child, a potential difficulty lies in the speed of speaking and the quality of enunciation. Most testers are undoubtedly aware of these hazards, and take the precaution of speaking both slowly and clearly. Many tests also require the tester to read each item twice, and this appears to be the standard procedure for attempting to ensure that the subject hears the question and knows what is required of him.

However, there are usually several or many testers used to test a given population and it is almost certain that no two will be identical in speed and clarity. Yet it is clear that the faster the speed of delivery, the less time there is for the learner to process what he hears. Also, the speed of speaking is interrelated with the syntax of the sentence. Two sentences of identical length can take significantly different times for the hearer to process. For example, sentence (1) takes longer for children to process at least through nine years of age (Kennedy, 1970).

    1. *She has less books than pens.*

    2. *She has more pens than books.*

While the two sentences take the same time to utter as part of the continuing stream of speech, the increased processing time required by the first sentence may cause certain subjects to lose track of subsequent parts of the utterance with a consequent breakdown in comprehension. (cf. Macnamara, 1967). This appears to be the case with comparatives, and it is only possible to guess at how widespread and far-reaching this may be across the whole range of syntactic complexity.

It should always be remembered that the comprehension of speech is largely on the speaker's terms, for it is he who determines the clarity, speed of delivery, and complexity of the sentences. Because the language development of young children to at least nine years is marked by highly individual rates of progress, the possibility of particular children not comprehending whole instructions is high, because they do not understand, or they take a long time to process one word or one part of a sentence.

In addition to this processing-time variable, there is another potential difficulty in speech perception which has its effect in particular with listeners who do not have a complete mastery of a language. This factor is the perception of function words. Function words in English are the two or three hundred words, including determiners, prepositions, auxiliaries, which are usually considered as being different from the open class of content words having greater lexical weight (nouns, verbs, etc.). Although function words constitute about half of all words we utter, they can be hard to hear because they are normally unstressed in English, and yet they are of crucial importance for comprehending. In the following examples, the effect of the underlined function word on the meaning of the sentence can be readily seen. Failure to hear the word in the stream of speech can result in faulty comprehension.

The price went UP 50 cents.
The price went UP TO 50 cents.
It's BEEN done.
It's BEING done.
Move TO the right.
Move IT TO the right.
Put the red block ONTO the table.
Put the red block UNDER the table.
If the last one WAS red, take a green one.
If the last one WASN'T red, take a green one.

Young children characteristically speak a form of English called telegraphese, omitting many function words, and it may be as late as ten years th'at full control of these semantically important words is achieved. Moreover, it should be noted that failure to hear a function word usually passes unnoticed. That is, a listener rarely knows when he has failed to hear such a word, whereas with content words, a listener is usually aware that he didn't *catch* the word and can ask for the sentence to be repeated.

If the child being tested is not a native speaker of Standard English, it is by no means inconceivable that when presented with a picture and told to *Point to the triangle under the line,* he hears *Put the triangle onto the line,* and reacts in bewilderment.

Even if a particular function word is heard, it is not certain that it will be interpreted correctly because of the importance of suprasegmental phenoma such as intonation and stress. For example, in a recent test of knowledge of concepts, children were given the following item; *See the cat* (points to the cat in the margin). *Point to the cat over here that is the same color.* If the tester hesitated in the middle of the sentence, it is possible that a young child or a nonnative speaker of the dialect of the tester would interpret *that* as a demonstrative rather than as a relative, i.e., *Point to the cat over here. That is the same color.* Confusion for the child would seem to be likely.

This paper has pointed out some ways in which children's test performance can be influenced by linguistic variables. It seems highly probable that the results of tests of aptitude and achievement with young children are frequently influenced in ways not directly related to the abilities being tested and, moreover, in an idiosyncratic manner. Much closer attention needs to be given to ensuring that the language of tests, particularly for young children, matches both on developmental and dialectal grounds the linguistic competence of the children being tested, and that children's abilities to perceive and process test instructions and items spoken by an adult are not overestimated.

REFERENCES

Beilin, H., and G. Spontak. "Active-Passive Transformations and Operational Reversibility." Paper read at S.R.C.D. meeting. Santa Monica, Calif.: 1969, unpublished.

Boehm, A. E. *Boehm Test of Basic Concepts.* (1969 ed.) New York: Psychological Corporation, 1969.

Braine, M., and B. Shanks. "The development of conservation of size." *Journal of Verbal Learning and Verbal Behavior,* 4 (1965), 227-42.

Brown, R., and J. Berko. "Word Association and the Acquisition of Grammar." *Child Development,* 31 (1960), 1-14.

Carroll, J. B. "Language Development in Children." *Encyclopedia of Educational Research.* New York: Macmillan, 1960.

Carroll, J. B. "Words, meanings, and concepts." *Harvard Educational Review,* 34 (1964), 178-202.

Cattell, R. B. *Culture Fair Intelligence Test.* Champaign, Ill.: Institution for Personality and Ability Testing, 1950.

Chomsky, C. The Acquisition of Syntax in Children from 5 to 10. M.I.T. Research Monograph No. 57, 1969.

Donaldson, M., and G. Balfour. "Less Is More: A Study of Language Comprehension in Children." *British Journal of Psychology,* 59 (1968), 461-71.

Entwisle, D., D. Forsythe, and R. Munso. "The Syntagmatic Paradigmatic Shift in Children's Word Associations." *Journal of Verbal Learning and Verbal Behavior,* 3 (1964), 19-29.

Ervin-Tripp, S. "Changes with Age in the Verbal Determinants of Word Association." *American Journal of Psychology* 74 (1961), 361-72.

Fodor, J. "Recent Developments in Psycholinguistics." Unpublished paper read at UCLA Graduate Linguistics Circle. 1969.

Hatch, E. "Four Experimental Studies in the Syntax of Young Children." Doctoral dissertation, UCLA, 1969, unpublished.

Hatch, E., J. Sheff, and D. Chastain. "The Five-year Old's Comprehension of Expanded and Transformed Conjoined Sentences." S.W.R.L. Technical Report No. 9, 1969.

Kennedy, Graeme D. "Children's Comprehension of English Sentences Comparing Quantities of Discrete Objects." Doctoral dissertation, UCLA, 1970, unpublished.

Labov, W., P. Cohen, C. Robins, and J. Lewis. A Study of Non-Standard English of Negro and Puerto-Rican Speakers. Cooperative Research Project No. 3288, 1968.

Macnamara, J. "The effects of instruction in a weaker language." *Journal of Social Issues,* 23 (1967), 120-34.

Menyuk, P. *Sentences Children Use.* M.I.T. Research Monograph No. 52, 1969.

Olds, H. F. *An Experimental Study of Syntactical Factors Influencing Children's Comprehension of Certain Complex Relationships.* Report No. 4, Harvard R and D Department, 1968.

Rothenberg, B. "Conservation of Number Among 4- and 5-year-old children: Some Methodological Considerations." *Child Development,* 40 (1969), 383-406.

Slobin, D. "Grammatical Transformations and Sentence Comprehension in Childhood and Adulthood." *Journal of Verbal Learning and Verbal Behavior,* 5 (1966), 219-27.

Tiegs, E. W., and W. W. Clark. *California Achievement Test.* Grades 1 and 2. Monterey, Calif.: California Test Bureau, 1957.

14. Are We Really Measuring Proficiency with Our Foreign Language Tests?

Eugène Brière

If we hope to be able to give minority children or anyone else good language education, we need to have valid and reliable methods of measuring language proficiency. To decide whether someone needs instruction in a language or how successful a particular language program has been, we need to be able to test how competent a child is in one or more languages. There are numbers of tests that claim or are believed to do just this, but in the following article, Eugène Brière points out the theoretical and practical weaknesses of the tests that are currently available. Professor Brière, associate professor of linguistics at the University of Southern California, is directing a project to develop tests in English as a second language for American Indian children. A portion of this paper was given at the seminar sponsored by the South East Asian Ministers of Education Organization in Bangkok, Thailand, in May 1970.

"Achievement" and "proficiency" in foreign languages mean different things to different people. In order to provide a common denominator for discussion I would like to start by giving operational definitions for both terms.

We will define "achievement" in language performance as the extent to which an individual student has mastered the specific skills or body of information which have been presented in a formal classroom situation. For example, an achievement test may be given to a class after the students have finished studying chapter X in book Y. Such a test may be designed to measure the degree of achievement acquired by the students of all, or part of, the phonological,

Reprinted from *Foreign Language Annals,* 4 (1971), pages 385-91, by permission of the author and the publishers.

morphosyntactic, and lexical categories which were first presented in chapter X. Presumably the teacher would be interested only in the degree of achievement of the information presented in chapter X and would not try to measure achievement of the material contained in chapter Z until this chapter was presented to the students in class.

"Proficiency" in a language is much more difficult to define and, obviously, much more difficult to measure in a testing situation. Proficiency is frequently defined as the degree of competence or the capability in a given language demonstrated by an individual at a given point in time independent of a specific textbook, chapter in the book, or pedagogial method. In other words, as defined by Harris[1] "a general proficiency test indicates what an individual is capable of doing now (as the result of his cumulative learning experiences)." One of the reasons that the term "proficiency" is much more difficult to define than the term "achievement" is the inherent notion of "degree of competence" in defining "proficiency." Are we talking about "linguistic competence," "communicative competence," or both? Furthermore, since language testing measures behavior, where can we find a model of behavior which we could use as a guide in designing a general proficiency test?

Perhaps a quick review of the development of language pedagogy and the subsequent testing instruments involved would be useful in understanding the problems in testing language proficiency and serve as a useful introduction to the current testing techniques reported here.

Over the past several years, different methods of teaching foreign languages or second languages have been used. In the beginning, language was considered synonymous with literature. Put differently, language was thought to consist of the printed words contained in books—preferably in books which had been written by prestigious authors. Consequently, classroom teaching consisted primarily of learning the writing system of the target language and then reading literary passages in the target language or translating these passages into the native language. When any attention was paid to anything other than translated prose, school programs were designed to provide memorization of verb paradigms or parsing of written sentences.

[1] David P. Harris, *Testing English as a Second Language* (New York: McGraw-Hill, 1969).

The tests or evaluation procedures developed from these literary-grammar-translation methods of teaching consisted of compositions and dictations in the target language or grammar translation exercises. Clearly, the scoring, evaluation, and grading used in the three techniques were subjective and made it difficult, or sometimes impossible, to assess the students' resulting performances in any systematic objective manner. Stylistics, spelling, and the examiner's personal prejudices frequently interfered with objective evaluation of achieved results and with reasonable predictions of success or failure in future learning in the target language. Since the variables of interest were not defined precisely, each examiner could use a different set of criteria for grading a composition or a translated passage. Some teachers placed more emphasis on grammatical precision (based, of course, on some literary style) while others were more concerned with imaginative, complex performances or stylistic considerations which showed "creativity" rather than simpleminded, grammatically precise inanities such as the "Look-Jane-Look" "See-the-ball" variety. Frequently, the net result was that fifteen or more different teachers could evaluate the same composition in fifteen or more different ways.

If any attention at all was given to developing oral proficiency in the target language, the ensuing "tests" frequently consisted of unstructured interviews or "oral compositions" which lead to the same chaotic conditions in evaluation as those described for the written tests.

After the structural linguists such as Fries and Lado[2] began to emphasize the primacy of proficiency in oral language, teaching methods and testing procedures changed considerably. For one thing, oral, structural pattern practice replaced the previous literary methods. "Discrete point" teaching and testing became the order of the day. What I mean by "discrete point" is the assumption that there are a number of specific things, the knowledge of which constitutes "knowing" a particular language, and that these things could be precisely identified at the different levels of syntax, morphology, and phonology. Lado, for example, using a paradigm developed by psychologists in paired associate learning to identify

[2]Charles C. Fries, *The Structure of English* (New York: Harcourt, 1952), Robert Lado, *Linguistics Across Cultures* (Ann Arbor: Univ. of Michigan Press, 1957).

proactive interferences, assumed that a contrastive analysis of the native language with the target language could precisely identify those learning problems which would be encountered by native speakers of L_1 attempting to learn a specific target language. Moreover, the learning problems identified through the procedure of contrastive analysis could be developed into discrete point teaching materials or tests by simply writing patterns or test items for each of the learning problems involved. In actual practice, however, the things which are thought to constitute a language are not frequently defined through contrastive analysis but more often through a structural analysis of the target language only. The ensuing identification of the phonemic contrasts, the morphemic privilege of occurrence in certain pattern slots, the vocabulary items and the contrasting sentence patterns which are to be taught and then tested are frequently chosen in a very arbitrary manner. TOEFL[3] is an example of a discrete item test which was definitely not based on contrastive analysis.

Perhaps the largest gain made in turning to discrete point testing was a specific identification of the categories to be tested and an objectivity in scoring which was possible with the translation or composition type of tests. Multiple choice items can be statistically analyzed for difficulty scores, discrimination scores, and correlations with external or internal criteria. We now have a method of reducing reliability and validity to a number which we can readily and easily understand. However, there is a growing concern among certain language test designers over the *actual* validity of this discrete point approach because of the very difficult problem of identifying precisely many of the complex variables which define the competence of a speaker or listener in any act of communication.

There is a growing agreement among psycholinguists and sociolinguists that traditional linguistic definitions of the notion of competence in a language are too narrow and are inadequate in identifying all of the skills involved when two people communicate. Consequently, discrete item language tests based on the narrow definition of linguistic competence will be inadequate. At best, such tests only give us some kind of measure of behavior which I will call

---

[3] Test of English as a Foreign Language produced by the Educational Testing Service, Princeton, N. J.

"surface" behavior based on the analogy of a floating iceberg. The part of the iceberg seen floating on top of the water is but a small fraction of what lies underneath the water. So it is with communicative competence. We suggest that the language tests being used today are limited to measuring that which is on the "surface" and can give us no information about what is "underneath." However, probably it is precisely these unidentified and unmeasured variables "underneath" which constitute the "bulk" of communicative competence. What is needed is a serious attempt to develop a model which will identify and measure those variables which, at the moment, are "underneath the surface." The remainder of this paper briefly summarizes some of the serious and sophisticated attempts currently being conducted in the United States.

In a recent paper, Bernard Spolsky,[4] University of New Mexico, suggested that although Fries rejected the layman's notion that knowing a certain number of words in a language constituted the criterion for knowing that language, he still maintained the related notion that knowing a language involves knowing a set of items. Spolsky suggests that testing of individual elements, such as sound segments, sentence patterns, or lexical items, is still inadequate. He points out that the layman's criterion for *knowing* a language is usually expressed in some type of *functional* statement. For example, "He knows enough French to read a newspaper and ask simple questions for directions." Statements such as these refer to language *use* and not to grammar or phonology. The question then arises, how does one go about deciding when someone knows enough language to carry out a specific function? One approach would be to give someone a language-using test to perform, such as having a physics major listen to a lecture on thermodynamics and then test the comprehension. Another approach would be to characterize the linguistic knowledge which correlates with the functional ability. However, one of the fundamental reasons that this approach has not proved successful is that it fails to take into account the fact that language is redundant and that it is creative.

---

[4]"What Does it Mean to Know a Language or How Do You Get Someone to Perform His Competence" *Language Learning and Language Teaching* Ed. Jack C. Richards and John W. Oller, Newbury House, 1972.

Redundancy (part of the statistical theory of communication) is present in all natural languages, since more units are used to convey a message than are theoretically needed. Spolsky has experimented with redundancy as a testing technique. In his experiments, noise was added to messages on tapes and the tapes were played to native and nonnative speakers. The nonnative's inability to function with reduced redundancy suggested that the missing key was the richness of knowledge of probability on all levels—phonological, grammatical, lexical, and semantic. At least two implications followed from these experiments. The first is that knowing a language involves the ability to understand a message with reduced redundancy. A model of understanding speech must then include the ability to make valid guesses about a certain percentage of omitted elements. The second implication is to raise some serious theoretical questions about the value of deciding a person knows a language because he knows certain items in the language. The principle of redundancy suggests that it will not be possible to demonstrate that any given language item is essential to successful communication, or to establish the functional load of any given item in communication. He makes the distinction between language-like behavior, for example, the utterances of a parrot, and knowing a language on the basis of creativeness, that is, the ability to produce and understand a sentence which may never have been heard before. One fundamental factor involved in the speaker-hearer's performance is his knowledge of the grammar that determined an intrinsic connection of sound and meaning for each sentence. We refer to this knowledge (for the most part, obviously, unconscious knowledge) as the speaker-hearer's "competence." Therefore, in searching for a test of overall proficiency, we must try to find some way to get beyond the limitation of testing a sample of surface features, and seek rather to tap underlying linguistic competence. Testing selected items can only give us a measure of surface behavior or performance.

Richard B. Noss,[5] with the Ford Foundation's English Language Center in Bangkok, Thailand, used an interesting technique which involved the students' own speech as interference and lack of redundancy factors. He instructed twenty-four Thai students to read three typewritten pages arranged in order of difficulty from easy to

_____
[5] Personal communication to the author.

hard. The students' responses were recorded. One week later, the students were asked to return and transcribe their own tapes in writing. Not only was the hierarchy of difficulty of the stimuli confirmed by their scores, but also it was clear that many of the students were unable to transcribe their own recordings perfectly. I suggest that not only did the students' recordings provide interference (even though they were listening to their own voices), but also that the factor of redundancy was lacking in their understanding of the target language.

John Upshur,[6] University of Michigan, feels that attempts to measure a "general proficiency factor" have been essentially unsuccessful primarily because of the lack of any performance theory generally available to, and useful for, those who might prepare production tests. He has suggested a simplified model which would specify some of the variables needed in a performance theory.

Upshur suggests that in the act of communication a Speaker's Meaning (SM) be distinguished from Utterance Meaning (UM) or Word Meaning (WM). In communication it is the task of the producer (a task certainly shared by the receiver or audience) to "induce" in or transmit to the audience a meaning (AM) which has as a part an equivalent of SM.

Because communication requires that AM contain SM, because UM is a medium through which this is accomplished, and because SM need not be equivalent, more is required than that S (and A) have competence in some language. For S to get his meaning across to A (i.e., to communicate to have AM contain SM), it is necessary (1) for A to get the word meaning, (2) for A to know the case relations for each W (this seems to be a part of UM), and (3) for A to get the relations between a proposition and other concepts.

Upshur then develops a model for A which could account for the processing of SM in A. The kinds of "components" in A which he suggests are such things as: perceptions of the outer world (PO); a store of concepts (AMs) resulting from the current communication transaction (CCS); a semantic net (NET); a linguistic competence (COMP) and several others.

---

[6]John A. Upshur, "Measurement of Oral Communication," in Heinrich Schrand, ed., *Leistungsmessung im Sprachunterricht* (Marburg/Lahn: Informationszentrum für Fremdsprachenforschung, 1969).

From S's point of view he must have a concept to communicate (SM), and some reason for doing so. S has the belief that A lacks the concept SM, and cares to have it. His communication ability is then a function of (1) his success in determining the constraints imposed by the contents of A's components, (2) his success in altering the contents of those components, and (3) his success (in language communication) in adapting his own competence.

The model suggests that oral production testing, viewed as one of the four skill components of the 1961 Carroll[7] model, is but one part of speaker communication testing. Communication measurement involves a matching of SM and AM, therefore "precise" measurement is not likely without comparable measures of both.

One experimental form to test one kind of communication situation has been and is being investigated by Upshur. In this technique, a set of thirty-six four-picture items was prepared. The S's specific task was to communicate to a remote A which one of the four pictures was identical to a single picture shown to him by an examiner. Students of English as a foreign language took the initial thirty-six item test and the utterances were recorded. Four native A's listened to the tapes. The interjudge reliability for correct items was .87. Uniformly high coefficients were found between raw scores, total response, and communication rate scores with composition and achievement test scores. (Incidentally, we are currently using a modification of this technique to elicit oral responses on our project to develop ESL proficiency tests for North American Indian elementary schoolchildren.)[8]

Leslie Palmer,[9] Georgetown University, has been experimenting with the evaluation of oral responses in English made by foreign students through the use of different elicitation techniques. He has his students read a story, paraphrase the story they have read, and tell a story about a holiday or festival in their own words. The responses elicited by the three different techniques are judged by trained members of his staff. The variation of degree of proficiency

---

[7]John B. Carroll, *Fundamental Considerations in Testing for English Language Proficiency of Foreign Students* (Washington, D.C.: Center for Applied Linguistics, 1961).

[8]English Language Testing Project sponsored by the Bureau of Indian Affairs, Washington, D.C.

[9]Personal communication to the author.

depending upon the *method* used for elicitation is unbelievably and discouragingly large.

Leon Jakobovits,[10] now at the University of Hawaii, points out that there is an obvious difference between linguistic competence as it is traditionally defined and communicative competence. The latter involves wider considerations of the communication act itself, considerations which the linguists have dismissed in their definitions of linguistic competence as being primarily the concern of paralinguistics, exolinguistics, sociolinguistics, and psycholinguistics. Since the authors of language tests are aware that the study of language *use* must necessarily encompass the wider competencies in communication competence, the development of language tests must move from the present position of measuring merely linguistic competence to the position of measuring communicative competence.

Jakobovits points out that speakers of a language have a command of various codes that can be defined as a set of restriction rules that determine the choice of phonological, syntactic, and lexical items in sentences. For example, the choice of address form in English, "using the title Mr. followed by the last name versus first name," is determined by the social variable which relates the status relation between the speaker and the listener. These selection rules and others of this type are as necessary a part of the linguistic competence of the speaker as those with which we are more familiar in syntax, such as accord in gender, number, and tense; and it would seem to be entirely arbitrary to exclude them from a description that deals with linguistic competence.

In order to be able to account for the minimum range of linguistic phenomena in communicative competence, it will be necessary to incorporate in the analysis three levels of meaning, namely linguistic, implicit, and implicative. By "linguistic meaning" Jakobovits refers to the traditional concerns of linguists such as Chomsky and Katz. This includes a dictionary of lexical meanings and their projection rules,' syntactic relations, and phonological actualization rules. By "implicit meaning" he refers to the elliptically derived conceptual event which an utterance represents. By this is meant that particular

---

10"A Fundamental Approach to the Assessment of Language Skills," in Jakobovits, *Foreign Language Learning: A Psycholinguistic Analysis of the Issues* (Rowley, Mass.: Newbury House, 1970).

implications for homonymous utterances are a function of the situational contents in which the utterance is used.

In order to recover the particular meanings of the word intended by the speaker, the listener must engage in an inferential process which makes use of his knowledge of the dictionary meaning of words as *well* as his knowledge of the overall situation to which the sentence as a whole refers.

"Implicative meaning" refers to the information in an utterance about the speaker himself, e.g., his intention, his psychological state, his definition of the interaction, etc. In some cases these implications are necessary to recover the intended meaning of the utterance. For example, "Do you have a match?" is not a question to be answered verbally, but a request for fire to light a cigarette.

The problem, then, of assessing language skills becomes the problem of describing the specific manner in which an individual functions at the three levels of meaning just identified. Language tests, then, must take into account the full range of phenomena in communicative competence if language *use* is to be tested.

Jakobovits makes some tentative suggestions with respect to some methodological approaches which may be used in connection with his classification scheme. Some of the methods suggested are:

A. *Judgments of acceptability*—ask a subject to judge the acceptability of an utterance or pick the most appropriate of two similar utterances.

B. *Semantic differential techniques*—subjects rate a word on a seven-point bipolar adjectival scale according to the Osgood method.

C. *Acting out situations*—ask a subject how he would say something under specified conditions in order to assess his encoding skills in terms of the different kinds of meaning just described.

Even scholars in the field of neurophysiological speech are beginning to question discrete point teaching, and presumably, discrete point testing. In a paper entitled "Physiological Responses to Different Modes of Feedback in Pronunciation Training," Richard Lee, Florida State University, reported some exciting experimental results to the TESOL conference in San Francisco in March 1970. Working on the premise that pattern drill and phonemic discrimination drill is *not* genuine language behavior, has *no counterpart* in natural language behavior, and produces boredom, lack of motivation, and little learning among the students, he performed the following experiment.

It has been established that some physiological arousal is necessary for learning to occur. Arousal is most often measured by heart rate, galvanic skin response, and breath rate. Of these measures, heart rate is the most robust. Ten women and eight men, all foreign students taking an ESL course, were measured on and E and M Physiograph Six. This machine is similar to the polygraph used in lie detector tests but free from connecting wires to a central recording machine, thus providing the student complete mobility. The heart rates of the students were measured at seven different points in time under two basic conditions: one was during normal conversation and the second was during pattern practice. The peaks of arousal which are expected during normal conversations did occur. Unfortunately, the measurements during pattern practice showed such little arousal in heart rate that Professor Lee was led to believe that no learning was occurring at all. In fact, the lines during pattern practice were almost flat with a slight drop at the seventh or last reading in time.

Admittedly, this is a small population from which to extrapolate to the universe, but I certainly hope he continues with this rather unusual technique for measuring learning in hopes that we can gain some insight into language teaching methods we are currently using.

The sociolinguistic works of Robert Cooper and Joshua Fishman, of Charles Ferguson and of William Labov (to name but a few) are providing language teachers, language testers, and linguists with data which could lead to that "breakthrough" which is now needed if we are to move ahead into an era of sophisticated understanding of what to teach and what to test in order to provide psychologically sound understanding of the complex variables involved in communicative competence.

Furthermore, I would like to conclude with my personal bias, which is that any *real* "breakthroughs" and new insights *must* be the results of an interdisciplinary team of teachers, testers, psychologists, sociologists, linguists, and many others. I can't think of any one single discipline (let alone a single person) which can provide all of the answers we now realize we need in order to provide new and exciting teaching materials and methods and truly valid test instruments to evaluate communicative competence.

15. The Limits of Language Education

Bernard Spolsky

When a scholar finds his field becoming relevant to the society in which he lives, he is easily tempted to assume he can cure all the ills he sees. Applied linguists are no exception; many have jumped from seeing how language education might help those who do not speak the standard language, to a belief that language problems are basic. Thus, in a recent article Garland Cannon (1971) speaks of the "original linguistic causes" of discrimination and seems to argue that the solution of "bilingual problems" will lead to a new millenium. Reading an article like this, one is reminded of the enthusiasm with which the new methods of language teaching were propounded in the fifties and early sixties: give us the money and the machines, we said, and the linguists will show you how to teach everyone a foreign language.

This belief in the existence of linguistic solutions explains linguists' disappointments when they find programs in English as a second language, or as a second dialect, or in bilingual education, being greeted with suspicion by the community for which they are intended. Serious-minded, honest, and well-intentioned applied linguists are discouraged when the NAACP condemns programs using Black English as part of an "insidious conspiracy" to cripple Black children ("Black Nonsense":, editorial in *The Crisis* [1971]) or when ESL programs are characterized as arrogant linguistic imperialism

This paper first appeared in *The Linguistic Reporter,* 13:3 (Summer 1971), pp. 1-5.

(editorial in *El Grito* [1968]). How can we be wrong, we ask, both when we try to recognize and preserve the child's language (as in bilingual or "bidialectal" programs) and when we try to teach the standard one (as in ESL or ESOD programs)?

The difficulty has arisen, I suspect, because linguists and language teachers have seen their task as teaching language: they have not realized that it is teaching students to use language. Thus, they have often ignored the place of language in the wider curriculum of school and in society as a whole. Take the example of literacy. We argue for adult literacy in English as a means of getting jobs, ignoring (or probably not knowing) that unemployment patterns are not controlled by linguistic but by economic and racial factors. A Mexican American is out of work not because he can't read, but because there is no work, or because the employers don't hire Mexicans.

It is important to distinguish between language as a reason and language as an excuse for discrimination. There are clearly cases in which someone's inability to use a language is a reason not to hire him; in such cases, teaching him the language will solve the problem. But there are many other cases in which language is used as an excuse, like race or skin color or sex, for not hiring someone. No amount of language training will change this, for the discrimination exists in the hearer and not the speaker. Blacks and Spanish Americans know this, but applied linguists and language teachers have often not noticed.

Exaggerated claims, then, are a part of the difficulty. But I do not suggest that applied linguists should, like some theoretical linguists, simply decide that their field has no immediate social relevance. It is important to see applied linguistics as one of the fields with a contribution to make, but at the same time to recognize clearly its limitations, for linguistic problems are a reflection of social problems rather than a cause. There is a linguistic barrier to the education of many children, but it is not the only barrier to social and economic acceptance.

The potential relevance of educational linguistics becomes more apparent if we look at language and language learning as part of the general school curriculum. There can be many views of the purpose of an educational system, but a central aim must be to make it possible for its graduates to take their place in society. To do this, they need to be able to control effectively the language of that society.

The society in which people live today is not a single entity. We all live in a great number of worlds: the world of our home, of our neighborhood, of our church group, of our occupations, of the culture that interests us. And it is often the case that these worlds or societies each have different languages or speech varieties. With the rapid expansion of scientific knowledge for example, whatever other language requirements an individual may have, he must have good control of one of the world's major languages if he wishes to keep up to date with modern physics. Again, however well he knows English, a child living in a New Mexican pueblo must be able to use the language of his people if he is to participate in the cultural and religious life of the kiva.

There are indeed people who live in a true monolingual situation and can attain complete self-realization in that language. Someone born in middle-class suburban America who, if he travels at all, does so as a tourist without understanding the cultures he is visiting, and who is satisfied with the culture provided by the television set and the newspaper, will no doubt be able to conduct his whole life in one language. Whatever his limitations, the advantages such a person has from life are denied to those who do not from the beginning master middle-class American English. To the extent that we believe that all people should have access to these opportunities, teaching English to those who speak other languages becomes a central responsibility of the American educational system; and not just to those who speak other languages, but also as is becoming increasingly clear, to those whose dialect is not acceptable.

This is not the time to enter into the question of the fundamental advantages or disadvantages of nonstandard dialects. Linguists seem reasonably convinced that no language or dialect is inherently inferior to any other, with the possible exception of pidgins. But we must also recognize political reality: there is no doubt that middle-class American culture assumes that its members will speak the standard language, and that it penalizes in various ways those who do not (Leibowitz, 1971). One of the first tasks of the educational system is to make it possible to overcome this disadvantage. This means that any American school must be aware of the language or dialect background of its students, and must make it possible for them to acquire the standard language as quickly as possible. There is good evidence to suggest that during this acquisition period other learning can take place in the child's first language. There is reason to believe for example that it is a wise strategy to teach a Spanish-speaking child to read in Spanish while he is busy acquiring English, or to teach a Navajo-speaking child to read in his own language first (Spolsky and Holm, 1971). This type of strategy leads to the sort of educational structure that William Mackey (1970), in his excellent typology, would classify as dual-medium bilingual education, which aims at acculturation and at shifting the students to the standard language gradually but as soon as possible.

But this so far assumes that everyone wishes, and should wish, to belong to a single monolithic English-speaking culture. This melting-pot hypothesis has now happily been replaced by an acceptance of cultural pluralism. In this case, the languages of the minorities must be recognized not just as something to be used during the transitional period, but as an integral part of the school curriculum.

But exactly what this part should be is still a matter for investigation. There are two basic strategies: to decide that each of the two languages concerned should have equal status throughout the curriculum, or to give them different status. The former strategy might well be considered in those cases where one is dealing with two languages each of which has a standard literature and each of which provides access to all aspects of culture, commerce, and science, e.g., French, English, Spanish. In the United States, this model has been proposed as the ideal by Gaarder (1970) and by other foreign-language teachers, and its implementation is the goal for the Dade County experiment in Florida. It has a number of special qualities. It assumes entry to the school system by two sets of students, each controlling a different language. During the initial period, English for the speakers of the X language is paralleled by teaching the other language to the speakers of English. The natural advantages that speakers of English would have over speakers of X is thus taken away: all students need to spend a large portion of their time acquiring a second language. The curricular cost is clearly large: the time spent on the second language is not available for other activities, but the presumed reward is a generation of educated bilinguals, equally at ease in two languages and cultures.

A great deal of attention has been paid to this model and particularly to the Dade County program. In Dade County, Florida, the bilingual program began in 1961 to deal with the influx of Cuban refugees. In its first approach, the program was transitional, paralleling teaching English as a second language with the use of Spanish-speaking Cuban teacher aides. In 1963, Coral Way Elementary School began a program in which all pupils, whether English or Spanish speaking, were taught half the day in each language. Since then, three more Dade County schools have followed the Coral Way pattern. Evaluation of Coral Way has been favorable, with data supporting the general conclusion that Cuban children are, by sixth grade, equally proficient in reading two languages. But no detailed evaluation has yet appeared. The major question that will need to be answered is the generalizability of the Coral Way experiment, with its Cuban middle-class children, its national spotlight, and its generous support, to situations where Spanish-speakers are less advantaged educationally and culturally.

One of the most thoroughly documented studies in bilingual education is another middle-class experiment. In the St. Lambert, Montreal, experiment (Lambert, Just, and Segalowitz 1970; Tucker 1971), a group of English-speaking parents asked for their children to be taught in French. After four years of the experiment, it is clear that the children have not suffered in educational achievement: their English measures are no worse than their peers taught only in English, and while they are not yet as good in French as native speakers, they do very well in it. Somewhat disappointingly, however, it has turned out that these children taught in French have no more favorable attitude to French Canadians than do other Montreal English Canadians, suggesting that neither language teaching nor teaching in a language leads to basic change in social attitude.

The second strategy for bilingual education is to regard the X language as a limited culture-carrying medium, and treat English as the main language of instruction. In this approach, the X language speakers use their own language for learning about their culture. In the first grades, X is used in the transfer classes, as a medium for concept development, and for learning to read. But even when the English as a second language program has reached its goal and the student can carry on with the main part of the curriculum in English, the X language remains the medium for cultural studies. In this model, then, we might have Spanish-speaking children learning to read in Spanish while learning English: when they move to a regular curriculum in English, they will still take a subject called Hispanic studies, taught in Spanish. It must be noted that this strategy is in fact one that maintains culture at the cost of maintaining isolation: the X speakers are the only ones capable of learning in the X language. This can presumably be overcome at the cost of having English-speaking children learn X. But note that we are then left with a monolithic "melting-pot" bilingual community, rather than two separate communities. The difficulties with this become clear when we consider a school with English and several X languages: if it is decided that *all* students must learn *all* the languages, there will be little time for anything else.

Almost all the programs funded under the Bilingual Education Program follow this strategy, as a result of the fact that they are almost all aimed at the first one or two grades of elementary school. Many proposals assume that the program will follow the present children through the system, but time will tell what comes of this. For it to happen, there will need to be major changes in teacher training and the preparation of a great deal of new instructional material.

Given present official concern for accountability, a great amount of evaluative data has been collected in the course of new programs. But so far, there has been no published work that permits objective assessment of the techniques and approaches. The two main studies of bilingual programs (Andersson and Boyer, 1970; John and Horner, 1971) were written too early to do much more than quote from evaluation proposals. It may be some time then before we have any clear evidence of the effectiveness of various approaches to teaching and using a language other than English in school.

What I have been saying about X languages also provides a model for dealing with X dialects. Even though a dialect may be nonstandard, it will still need recognition as a potentially viable medium during the phase when the standard dialect is being taught. The possibility of maintenance for cultural purposes is presumably available, but it is unlikely to be chosen simply because the nonstandard dialect is generally not regarded as a valuable culture transmitter.

The American situation then calls both for English as a second language and bilingual education. A child coming to school must be taught the standard language if he is to have access to the general culture and economy. At the same time, he has a right to be taught in his own language while he is learning enough English to handle the rest of the curriculum. Communities that wish to maintain their own cultures and language may opt for this, recognizing the values and costs: separateness, and less time for "marketable" education. Communities that wish for a new blend of cultures may choose this, paralleling the teaching of English as a second language with the teaching of the second language to the English speakers. Establishing a language education policy like this will not solve society's ills: it won't overcome racial prejudice, or do away with economic and social injustice. But it will be a valuable step in this direction and a contribution of linguistics to society.

REFERENCES

Andersson, Theodore, and Mildred Boyer. *Bilingual Schooling in the United States.* 2 vols. Washington, D. C.: GPO, 1970.

Cannon, Garland. "Bilingual Problems and Developments in the United States." *PMLA,* 86 (1971), 452-58.

Fishman, Joshua, and John Lovas. 1970. "Bilingual Education in Sociolinguistic Perspective." *Tesol Quarterly,* 4. (1970), 215-22.

Gaarder, Bruce A. "The First Seventy-six Bilingual Education Projects." *Report of the Twenty-First Annual Round Table Meeting on Linguistics and Language Studies.* 23. Washington, D. C.: Georgetown University Press, 1970, 163-78.

John, Vera P., and Vivian M. Horner. *Early Childhood Bilingual Education.* New York: MLA, 1971.

Lambert, W. E., M. Just, and N. Segalowitz. 1970. "Some Cognitive Consequences of Following the Curricula of the Early School Grades in a Foreign Language." *Report of the Twenty-First Annual Round Table on Linguistics and Language Studies.* 23. Washington, D. C.: Georgetown University Press, 1970, 229-79.

Leibowitz, Arnold H. *Educational Policy and Political Acceptance.* ERIC Clearinghouse for Linguistics, 1971.

Mackey, William F. "A Typology of Bilingual Education." *Foreign Language Annals,* 3 (1970), 596-608.

Spolsky, Bernard, and Wayne Holm. "Literacy in the Vernacular: The Case of the Navajo." *Studies in Language and Linguistics 1970-71.* Ed. Jacob Ornstein and Ralph W. Ewton, Jr. El Paso: Texas Western Press, 1971.

Tucker, Richard C. "Cognitive and Attudinal Consequences of Following the Curricular of the First Few Grades in a Second Language." Paper read at the TESOL Convention, 1971.